MW01042326

SOLDIER UNDER THREE FLAGS

Exploits of Special Forces' Captain Larry A. Thorne

SOLDIER UNDER THREE FLAGS

Exploits of Special Forces' Captain Larry A. Thorne

by

H. A. Gill, III

Pathfinder Publishing
Ventura California U.S.A.

SOLDIER UNDER THREE FLAGS

Copyright © 1998 by H. A. Gill, III

All rights reserved. No part of this book may be reproduced or transmitted in any form or by any means, electronic or mechanical, including photocopying, recording or by any information storage and retrieval system without written permission from the authors, except for the inclusion of brief quotations in a review.

Pathfinder Publishing of California
458 Dorothy Avenue
Ventura, CA 93003
(805) 642-9278

Library of Congress Cataloging-in-Publication Data

Gill, H. A. (Henry A.), 1955-
    Soldier under three flags : exploits of Special Forces' Captain
Larry A. Thorne / by H. A. Gill, III.
        p. cm.
    Includes bibliographical references and index.
    ISBN 0-934793-65-4 (softcover)
    1. Törni, Lauri Allan, 1919-1965. 2. United States. Army.
Special Forces--Officers--Biography. 3. Soldiers--Finland-
-Biography. 4. Finns--United States--Biography. 5. Finns--Germany-
-Biography. I. Title.
U53.T63G55 1998
356' . 167'092--dc21
[B]   98-4602
                                                          CIP

DEDICATION

To my wife, Yun-Hee and son, Henry. She drove me and believed in me when I got discouraged and he kept me historically accurate and entertaining. My eternal gratitude to you both.

ACKNOWLEDGEMENTS

This book would not have been possible without the assistance of many others who need to be recognized. If I missed anyone, it certainly wasn't for trying. While in no order of importance, I am most grateful to the following people and organizations who gave of their time and effort.

American:

Risto Marttinen, John Larsen, Mike Phelan, Fred Fuller, David Hackworth, Bill Dillingham, Charlie Rhodes, Jimmy "Blue Eyes" Dean, Dick Bishop, Les Ristinen, Nils Lucander, David Kauhaahaa, John Plaster, Bob Rheault, Don Lassen, Danny Brosnan, Joe Quade, Ed Siergiej, Mel Therrien and the soldiers of the 10th Special Forces Group (Airborne).

Finnish:

President (Emeritus) Mauno Koivisto, LTC Lars Rönnquist, Kaija Mikkola, Jarl Tornquist, the Lindholm-Ventola Family, Agneta Lindroos-Pitkänen, Paavo Kairinen, CAPT Jukka Paijala, LTC Raimo Vertanen, LTC Osmo Hakkarainen, MAJ Kari Vainio, the surviving members of the Osasto Törni and the members of the Finnish Airborne Guild ("Jääkärit!).

To all of the authors whose previous works I have poured over to understand the story along the way. To the late SGM

Bill Pawlick and CPT Larry Dring, "Friends, I wish that you were here to share in the triumph." Finally, I'd like to thank my publisher, Mr. Eugene Wheeler, Pathfinder Publishing, who believed in me and gave me this opportunity.

CONTENTS

PREFACE

One day in the early 1970s, while a cadet at The Citadel, I was re-reading Robin Moore's novel, *The Green Berets* between classes when I was surprised by two of my instructors. The two Special Forces sergeants, MSGT Bill Pawlick and SFC Jim Wheeler stopped to ask what I was reading and asked if I enjoyed the book. I replied that some of it seemed a bit far-fetched; especially one character—Sven Kornie. Sharing knowing glances and a short laugh with each other, MSG Pawlick told me, "They all existed, especially old Larry Thorne" suggesting that Kornie was patterned after Thorne. Then, MSG Pawlick told me that it would be quite a tale if anyone could piece Thorne's life together. That simple challenge led me on this journey of piecing together stories of Thorne's life for the next 23 years.

Intrigued, I checked the chapter about Sven Kornie again. In the book, it said that Kornie was a Finn, had won every medal for bravery that Finland could bestow, disappeared for an extended period of time and eventually surfaced in the US Army Special Forces. I wanted to know more, to somehow bring this fictional character to life.

Several days later I ran into another friend of mine, Captain Larry Dring. Knowing that Captain Dring had a wild reputation in Special Forces, I asked Larry if he knew about a Captain Larry Thorne. "Of course," he said, "Almost everyone knows or knows of Larry Thorne. He was a part of a group of Finns who came to this country to fight the Russians. Darn fine soldier." I asked whatever happened to Thorne and Dring said that he really didn't know. By the vague answer and the trailing off of his voice, I knew not to pursue Thorne's fate any further with Captain Dring.

Still, I wanted to know. I made a point of seeing MSG Pawlick in his office one day. In those days, MACV-SOG operations were still highly classified. I asked MSG Pawlick, "Top, I know that you did some weird shit in Vietnam, was this Larry Thorne part of C&C, (Command and Control)?" MSG Pawlick quickly looked around the room and then leaned across the desk while motioning for me to come closer. "Hank," he said quietly, "You're asking about shit that you shouldn't be. Maybe one of these days, it will be possible for me to tell you about it." Suffice it to say that SFC Jim Wheeler was even more blunt when I asked him, but he did give me a big, all-knowing smile and a wink.

Not until 1982 did I ever get any answers to my questions. Many people that I asked said that they either knew or knew of Thorne; however, nobody would give me anything of real substance. My numerous letters to Finland went unanswered. Finally, I was able to contact a Finnish Captain Jukka Paijala who provided a great deal of information about Thorne. Captain Paijala opened a number of doors for me and I began to contact many of Thorne's former comrades. It began to snowball. Finns are a reserved and quiet people who don't trust easily. Through various introductions and letters, the Finns eventually warmed to me and shared their knowledge.

It is difficult to become a legend in one's own army, but what sort of special person becomes a legend in two armies? As impossible as that might seem, Larry Thorne did exactly that by winning every medal for valor which his native Finland could bestow and by legendary service in the US Army Special Forces. In all of the years of interviewing his comrades or reading documents, I have yet to meet anyone who spoke ill of him. The closest I ever came to a harsh word was the admonition that it should be remembered that he was merely a man, not a god or an idol. That advice was a constant companion while writing this book, a book which is the product of 24 years of curiosity and nagging questions which I couldn't leave alone.

Someone once said that truth is stranger than fiction. Whoever said that surely must have known about Lauri Törni/Larry Thorne. A fiction writer would have been challenged to come up with such a twisting and turning plot and still remain believable. His life, from humble beginnings, was one incredible adventure after another. I recall that one author stated that military history shouldn't be read in a warm home, sitting in a favorite chair with a steaming cup of hot coffee nearby. Instead, he argued, military history should be read when one is cold, wet, hungry and so tired that they have trouble staying awake, to truly understand the story. This book is not the case, but the reader should be ready for an incredible journey. I hope that you will enjoy reading it as much as I have enjoyed following the trail to write it. And so, the circle begins...

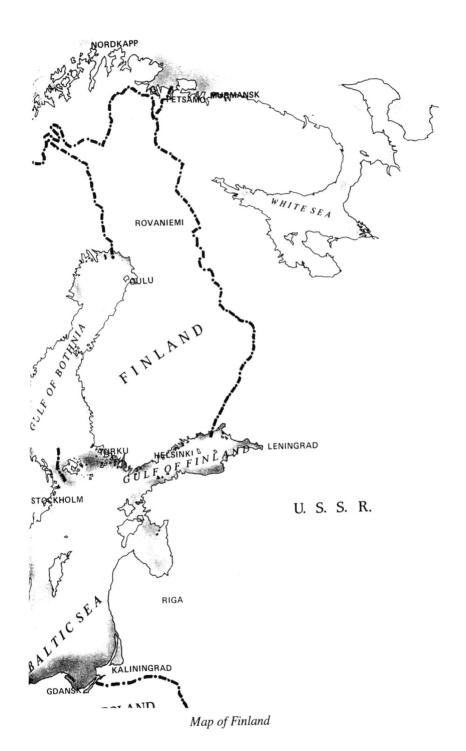

Map of Finland

1

THE RAILWAY STATION

At a nondescript, Finnish railway station not far from the front lines, a small group of Finnish soldiers gathered around a glowing potbellied stove while seeking shelter from the cold of a typical Finnish winter day. They were waiting for the train which would take them back to their homes for a few days of well deserved leave, a chance to forget the hard fighting which they had participated in only hours and days before. The small room was crowded. The only sounds were the crackle of the fire, a cigarette being lit, an occasional conversation, a muffled laugh and an odd explosion in the distance. The soldiers had thoughts of home and a silent prayer of thanks.

Bundled up in a woolen greatcoat and sleeping in a chair propped against the wall in the corner of the room was their leader. A man, only a few years older than themselves, but one who they trusted with their very lives. The young man's chiseled features were covered by the collar drawn tight around his face. His cap was drawn down covering his closely cropped blond hair and striking blue eyes while his large, rough hands were thrust deeply into the warmth of his jacket pockets. No insignia or rank was visible on his common Finnish Army gray greatcoat. Had he been awake, an observer might have noted that the young man was around 5' 11" tall, was solidly muscled and weighed 165 lbs. His features were typically Nordic. He looked vaguely like the movie celebrity Hardy Kruger. The strain of recent combat was apparent on his 24 year old face which had only a small sprouting of whiskers from his upper lip and chin. Despite his young age, he was a professional soldier and a man to be reckoned with.

The serenity of this scene was shattered by the opening of the door and the howling of the winter wind. The cold blast of the Arctic air made everyone unconsciously shiver as the stranger entered the room noisily. After a brief moment, the stranger looked around the room and began to bellow, "What are you men doing in here? This is the officer's room, all of you men, outside, now! Get outside, now." Despite murmured grumbles, the soldiers tightened their coats around them and began to shuffle outside to stand in the cold on the open train platform. Everyone that is, except for the nondescript young soldier sleeping in the chair in the corner. All of the commotion had failed to wake him. Or so it seemed.

The stranger, a major, continued to bellow for the soldiers to hurry and get out. His attention was immediately drawn to the one soldier who didn't obey his rantings. Walking over to the sleeping soldier, the major once more yelled for him to leave. Without looking up, the soldier was heard to say, "You're making too much goddamned noise. It is getting hard to sleep around here!" In a moment of absolute fury, the major pushed the sleeping soldier and screamed for him to come to attention.

After several shoves the stocky soldier stood up and contemptuously looked at the major. The enlisted soldiers watched through the open door knowing what was about to happen. The now awakened soldier announced, "I am Luutenatti Lauri

Törni and I am trying to sleep! You are making too much goddamned noise!" With that, the young lieutenant knocked the major unconscious with a single punch of his fist. He then unceremoniously dumped the flaccid major into another chair, motioned for his enlisted soldiers to come back inside, and proceeded to go back to sleep.

Hours later in a cramped military stockade, a Finnish Military Police sergeant answered the ringing telephone. "Yes," he said, "We have all of those men in custody and the major is pressing charges. No, sir, they are in jail, we can't release them. But sir...."

Lieutenant Törni and his men were soon delivered back to the front, their leave now a forgotten dream. No charges were ever filed, no court-martial was ever performed, and the whole incident became a sort of inside joke in the unit. Törni and his men, the jaegers, were needed immediately at the front. Shortly after their release from the stockade, they were locked in desperate combat with their mortal enemies, the Red Army. Finland needed her best soldiers at the front and was more than willing to turn a blind eye to a momentary transgression.

Lauri Törni (3rd from right) and his counter-reconnaissance company. Finland, summer 1943. (Courtesy of Petri Sarjanen).

2

SIMPLE BEGINNINGS

L auri Allan "Lasse" Törni was born in Viipuri (Vyborg), Finland on 28 May 1919. He was the oldest surviving boy of Rosa and Jalmari Törni, and had two sisters: Salme (born 1921) and Kaija (born 1922). An older brother, Unto Sven, was born in January 1918 but tragically died during a smallpox epidemic the following June. The Törnis were a tight-knit and loving family—a refuge against the world. His father, Jalmari, was a ship's captain for the Finnish Sugar, Limited shipping lines who made a living delivering sugar from Viipuri to other Finnish ports such as Helsinki, Turku or Vasa.

Törni attended the Viipuri Grammar School from 1926 until 1934. While never a brilliant student, he was described as a natural leader when it came to the other boys of his childhood. He was an adventuresome boy, who was frequently into something. Lasse Törni was reserved and quiet; yet, he could be charming and genial in nature. To those unfamiliar with these traits, Törni's long periods of silence were sometimes mistaken for sullenness or anger; however, this was often not the case. These traits carried on into his later life where friends said that it was always easy to laugh with Törni and hard to get upset with him despite his periodic outrageous antics. Sometimes, his father took him on cruises to other Finnish ports and taught his son about the sea. Little could the young Lauri know how valuable that knowledge would be in later life. To him, it was just another chance for adventure. Yet, to paraphrase the late author Louis L'Amour, adventure is just another name for trouble.

L - R Lauri, Salme and Kaija (seated) Törni, Viipuri, Finland.

L - R Jalmari, Lauri, Salme, and Rosa Törni. Kaija is seated.

The Törni family lived in the Finnish city of Viipuri, in the district known as Hiekka. The ancient Swedish Viipuri Castle, the Old Town, and the medieval defenses were visible from the Törnis' residence. As a native of Viipuri, Törni was keenly aware of the historical significance of his hometown in Finnish history. Viipuri, also known as Vyborg, had been built around a Swedish castle in 1293 A.D. It had withstood numerous invasions over the years but was finally captured by the army of Peter the Great of Russia in 1710. It was ceded to Russian control by the terms of the Treaty of Nystad in 1721. Finland was annexed as a Grand Duchy in 1809 by Tsar Alexander I and Viipuri Province was returned to local Finnish administration in 1812. Finland eventually won its independence from Imperial Russia in 1917. To the Finns, the ancient fortress city of Viipuri was both a symbol and a reminder of the traditional invasion routes and ancient, deep-held animosities towards the Russians.

As with many young men, Törni wasn't sure of what he wanted to do with his life. At the urgings of his parents, he attended the Viipuri Business High School from September 1936 to May 1937, but never obtained a diploma. Additionally, he worked as a helper in a tool shop. Despite these preparations, he never could see himself as a businessman. Some unknown force was always beckoning him. But what?

While still in High School, Törni joined the Finnish Civic Guards (Suojeluskunta) which is separate from the Regular and Reserve Finnish Army units, and is similar to the U.S. National Guard. The Civic Guards was a voluntary organization which fostered peacetime activities such as rifle and skiing competitions; athletics, and concerts. At the time he joined, approximately 80,000 to 100,000 other Finns were members. During wartime, the Civic Guards were to augment the regular army, as well as to train recruits and perform civil defense duties. Due to the lack of paved roads and long, snowy winters, the Finns became skilled cross-country skiers as children. In the Civic Guards, Törni excelled as a skier, marksman, and athlete. He enthusiastically participated in a new sport called "orienteering" which required the competitors to race through unfamiliar territory in any weather aided only by a compass and map. Many of these competitions were further complicated by being held at night in the dense Finnish forests. Törni's expert navigational skills, excellent physical conditioning, and ability to ski cross-country, along with a knowledge of the forest, made him a fierce competitor.

At 19 years of age in 1938, Lauri Törni was called up for his compulsory one year of national service in the Finnish Regular Army. As a child, he enjoyed associating with local soldiers and once obtained some extra cartridges which he detonated with great glee to the consternation of many others. He eagerly reported for duty and began training in the skills which would be his profession for the rest of his life. Törni attended his Basic Infantry Training Course at Kiviniemi, Finland and was assigned to the 4th Jaeger Infantry Battalion (JP4). After serving his compulsory time, Törni was discharged on 16 November 1939, but soon reenlisted in the regular army as the tensions between Finland and the Soviet Union grew. Many of his superiors were impressed with the young soldier's abilities. Törni was soon promoted to Corporal and attended the Finnish Non-Commissioned Officer's (NCO) academy and a veterinarian NCO academy.

By 1939, the storm clouds of war began to gather. Emboldened by the recent signing of a Non-Aggression Pact with Germany and the absorption of the Baltic States of Lithuania, Estonia, and Latvia, along with a portion of Poland, the Soviet Union became extremely aggressive towards Finland. The Soviet Union, in a move to obtain a larger buffer zone in case the West should attack, made three enormous demands for territory upon Finland. The first demand was that Finland lease the strategic Hanko Cape to the Soviet Union for a period of thirty years. The next two demands were that

Finland cede the northern port of Petsamo and the entire Karelian Isthmus to the Soviet Union. Being a sovereign nation, the Finns could never agree to such demands and tried further negotiations. Besides, had the Finns ceded to the Soviet Union's demands, they would have been in a worse strategic position than they were already. The Finns, with their mistrust of the Soviets and their rejection of Communism, felt that they were an isolated and exposed outpost of Western civilization. They saw themselves as a democratic bulwark against Bolshevism and were certain that the countries of the West would ultimately support them.

The Soviet Union confidently began to badger and bully Finland with wild accusations and border incidents. Finally, on 28 November 1939, the Soviet Union broke off negotiations and the stage was set for war. Soviet Foreign Minister Molotov then denounced the non-aggression pact with Finland. "Russia could no longer stand the unbearable situation which the hostility of the Finns has forced upon the poor Soviets," he said. Molotov then immediately ordered the armed forces of the Soviets to be ready for an 'emergency.' So confident were the Soviets of their bluff that a rising young commissar named Nikita Kruschev later recalled, "We thought that all we had to do was raise our voice a little bit. If that didn't work, we would fire one shot and the Finns would put up their hands."

But, Finland defiantly stood its ground. Following an intense 30 minute artillery barrage along the entire front, four Soviet armies of 16 divisions supported by 1,700 tanks and artillery, stormed across the Finnish border on 30 November 1939. A British officer, assigned to the embassy, was reported to have joked that Finland had to loot their national museums for artillery. The Soviets, having secretly built roads through the dense forests in preparation for the war, were able to move more rapidly than the Finns had anticipated. Expecting an easy conquest and a welcome by liberated Finnish workers, the Soviets were stunned by the ferocious Finnish defense. The warlike spirit and ancient animosities of the Finns were awakened by the Russians. Finnish war cries which harkened back to the Thirty Years War such as "Hakkää päälle!" (Cut them down!) were soon heard across the battlefields as the Finns made their displeasure known. According to the author William R. Trotter in his book, *A Frozen Hell:*

> *Most Finnish units found themselves in action literally on their home ground (or) terrain very similar to land...known since childhood...Officers were usually well known to their men from peace time and were often addressed by their first names or nicknames during combat. There was probably less spit and polish than in any other army in Europe. Finnish troops knew they were in the army to fight, not to march in parades..*

30 November 1939 found Törni, now a field mess and veterinary NCO, along with JP4, stationed near the city of Rautu on the Karelian Peninsula. The Finnish Army had organized 21,500 men into four groups (U, M, L & R) in forward positions ahead of the main defenses of the Mannerheim Line. Törni and JP4 were part of Group R on the northern flank of the Finnish defensive line. Törni vividly remembered his first combat experience:

> *We had realized for several months that the Russians were going to attack and I was with a light infantry battalion on the Russian border. One morning while we were having breakfast, about 5:30 or 6 o'clock, we heard heavy artillery fire many kilometers to the south.*
>
> *At first we thought it was some kind of practice, but a few minutes later they started putting the same*

*type of heavy concentration on our area and we
realized it was for real.*

*But we were laughing and joking about it until a
round came in and hit close to me and I saw a
friend's insides falling out on the snow. After that,
I didn't laugh anymore.*

*Finnish machine gun position, Finland. (Courtesy of Nils Lucander, via
John Larsen).*

*Two Finns in defensive position armed with Soviet DP38 light machine
gun and Suomi submachine gun. (Courtesy of Nils Lucander).*

It was a long time before Törni laughed again. He and Group R gave a spirited account of themselves in the battle with the Soviets at Rautu. The Finns only gave ground when they ran out of ammunition. Using the terrain to their advantage, the Finnish Army slowly retreated towards the Mannerheim Line in a manner they had practiced prior to the war. They left nothing of value or use to the Soviets in their wake. By expertly using Finland's 60,000 lakes, along with thick forests, marshes, swamps, and rivers to their advantage, the Finns forced the Red Army units into areas where they could be isolated and outflanked. Finnish snipers, grudgingly named '**cuckoos**' by the Russians, harassed the attackers mercilessly. On skis, camouflaged with white capes, the Finns sought to outflank, isolate, surround, and then annihilate Red Army units in a tactic called '*mottis*' (woodpiles). And pile them up they did. Sergeant Törni's battalion commander, Lieutenant Colonel Matti Aarnio gained the nickname, "Motti-Matti" for his superb skill in surrounding and annihilating superior Red Army units. The Finns struck terror into the Red Army units, many of them composed of conscripted peasants, Ukrainians who were unsuited for winter warfare. The Red Army was roadbound and dreaded the dense Finnish forests which they called, '**White Death**.'

Finland's weather was a tremendous ally. Since 1828, only two other winters had been colder than the winter of 1939-1940. Temperatures of minus 20 to minus 40 degrees Fahrenheit with freezing rain, snow, and ice were common. The deep snow hindered all movement except by skis. In the summer, the earth turns to quagmires of mud while the temperature sometimes soars as high as 80 degrees Fahrenheit. Summer also brings out clouds of blood-thirsty mosquitoes to harass the unprotected. Besides the mind-numbing cold, the Scandinavian midnight sun and endless days of darkness sapped morale on both sides. Faced with such unexpected resistance and a terrible climate, the Red Army became an international laughingstock as the Finns inflicted terrible losses upon them. William R. Trotter wrote:

The butchery was dreadful. In a number of cases, Finnish machine gunners had to be evacuated due to stress...after becoming emotionally unsuitable from having to perform such mindless slaughter, day after day.

The Russians attempted to keep the truth of their Finnish campaign hidden from the world. "Stalin was not pleased."

By the end of December, Leningrad was threaded, several times a day by long slow trains, their windows covered with curtains, filled to suffocation with maimed, starving, frostbitten Red Army troops...Leningrad's regular hospitals were swamped; by mid-December so were the emergency wards that had been set up in schools and factories. By Stalin's birthday (December 21), the long grim trains no longer even stopped in Leningrad but rolled eastward all the way to Moscow.

Meanwhile, Törni and his Finns were highly mobile and used their skis to cover long distances to strike where the Soviets least expected. The Finns used their mobilty to continually counter the Soviet's numerical advantage. Time and again, the Finns would silently ski up on a Russian force, quickly kick off their skis at the last minute and attack at close range with their excellent Suomi submachine guns, grenades, rifles, and their deadly puukko knives. Lacking in technology and modern weapons, the Finns used simple methods to counter the Soviet's numerical advantage. To channel the Soviets into ambushes, the Finns strung barbed wired between trees which was quickly covered by snow. The world was introduced to "Molotov Cocktails," bottles filled with gasoline and other chemicals which were used to burn Soviet tanks. Having few anti-tank weapons, the Finns used their Molotov cocktails, satchel charges of explosives, and sometimes even jammed logs into the tracks to destroy or disable Soviet tanks.

The Finns also developed "Abattis," or traps of fallen trees to block Soviet tanks on the narrow forest roads. They also became experts in booby-traps and land mine warfare. As the Finns retreated, they destroyed or burned everything of value to the advancing Soviets and booby-trapped things which would appeal to the Soviet peasant soldiers. Watches and doorways were booby-trapped. Finnish land mines created fear and panic in the Red Army, and made them extremely hesitant and cautious. German General Erfurth later wrote:

The strength of the Finnish soldier lies in individual combat. The Finns possess an infallible instinct for finding their way in the dense growth of the pathless woods. Nothing is heard or seen of Finnish troops whether resting or marching, even from the closest proximity. Terrain training is of a very high order. A special technique for movement through the woods has been developed and practiced so that the troops advance quickly, in the right direction and without losing contact. A Finnish company moves in the primeval forest just as smoothly and unerringly as a German company in the open landscape of central Europe. All Finns are enthusiastic hunters and sports lovers and fighting wakens in them all their hunting instincts. The aggressiveness of the troops is very keen. Their achievements in long-range combat patrolling cannot be surpassed.

Finnish soldier with Suomi submachine gun takes aim at the Russians. (Courtesy of Nils Lucander, via John Larsen).

Finnish sentry on guard duty during the Winter War. Armed with Suomi submachine gun. (Courtesy of Nils Lucander, via John Larsen).

Sergeant Törni distinguished himself in the battles of Rautu and Lemetti. During the Winter War (1939 - 1940), Törni served with JP4, Independent Infantry Battalion 8 (ErP 8) and Independent Infantry Battalion 18 (ErP 18). Near Lemetti, all of Törni's immediate officers were killed or disabled in the fierce fighting. Törni's unit was holding a small hill, nicknamed the "Sugar Loaf" which dominated the terrain and overlooked a particularly critical road junction. If the Soviets seized "Sugar Loaf," their tanks would cut off the Finnish forces from reinforcement. Both sides knew how crucial that small hill was. The fighting was intense as the Soviets attempted to seize control of the hill and cut the Finns' lines of communication. Panic set in and the Finns seriously considered surrendering. At this crucial moment, Törni, then the mess sergeant, arrived on the scene and took command. He reorganized the defenses, gave spirit to the defenders and then set out to reestablish communications with higher headquarters. Törni ordered the Finns to hold out until his return and then skied out of the defensive perimeter following the severed communications wire towards Soviet positions.

At Törni's command headquarters, the staff frantically attempted to regain communications with the defenders of the "Sugar Loaf." The position must be held at all costs. Suddenly, Törni entered the command tent and made his critical report regarding the situation at the "Sugar Loaf." The Finnish officers and staff were astounded by the young sergeant's actions and miraculous appearance. Törni had successfully skied through both the Soviet's positions and past the numerous Finnish sentries without being detected. After making his report, Törni returned to "Sugar Loaf" with his new orders. Repeating his incredible performance, he again passed through both Soviet and Finnish lines without incident. With communications once more established, Törni directed the Finnish defenses against the Soviet assaults. When a nearby position, defended by Swedish-speaking Finns began to waiver, Törni

Simple Beginnings

realized the tactical importance and skied to their position from the "Sugar Loaf." Although he didn't speak Swedish, Törni took command, and through gestures, shouts, curses, and punches successfully defended the position. Once more, he returned to the "Sugar Loaf" through Soviet lines. The 20 year old mess sergeant's bravery saved the day.

A short time later Sergeant Törni led the first penetration of the encircled Soviet 18th Yaroslav Division and the 54th Tank Brigade. In the ensuing battle, the Soviets were annihilated and 405 tanks were put out of action. In February 1940, Törni participated in the near total destruction of the Soviet 168th Division in the "great motti" running from Kitela to Koirioja near Lake Ladoga. Fierce battles in the winter darkness raged as half of the 168th Division was destroyed by the encircling Finns, but the desperate Soviets were able to break through by early March 1940 and escape. During the breakthrough, several Finnish infantry companies were annihilated in the intense fighting.

Again, Törni's superiors recognized that he was an excellent combat soldier and leader. In February 1940, he was pulled from combat and sent to Reserve Officer's School at Niinisalo, Finland. Törni was fortunate since he was one of only 200 men of the original 1,200 men of JP4 to survive the Winter War.

Despite the Finns' fierce resistance, the Red Army finally pierced the Mannerheim Line on 11 February 1940. Their defenses crumbled as the Red Army rushed towards Viipuri. While the average Finnish soldier believed that they were winning the war, their leaders in Helsinki knew otherwise. The Finnish government, faced with a national catastrophe, opted for a negotiated peace. On 13 March 1940, Finnish President Kallio signed an armistice and cabled it to Moscow, paraphrasing the Old Testament Book of Zachariah 11:17, "May the hand wither which is forced to sign such a

31

paper." Five months later, President Kallio's right arm was paralyzed by a stroke. He was dead within the year.

As a last insult, which the Finns have not forgotten nor forgiven, the Red Army let loose a fierce barrage of artillery and aerial bombing on 13 March 1940 just an hour and fifteen minutes before the armistice. To the Finns, this act was vengeful and pure spite. Moscow finally signed the armistice which ended the Winter War on 20 March 1940. The world news reported that evening:

> *The whole world tonight realizes that the terms of the Russo-Finnish treaty are even worse than we thought they might be. The cost of peace to the Finns is heavy and bitter.*

For 105 days, the Finnish Army stood alone and humiliated the massive Red Army. Finland killed some 175,000 - 200,000 Russians and wounded approximately 200,000 to 300,000 at the cost of 23,000 Finnish dead. It should be remembered that Finland also suffered another 10,000 permanently injured along with 35,000 wounded—this from a population of only 3.5 million.

But now, it was Finland's turn to be humiliated and humbled. According to the peace plan, Finland had to cede approximately 16,100 miles of territory to the Soviet Union. The new boundaries between the Soviet Union and Finland were roughly the ones established by the Treaty of Nystad in 1721. Some 420,000 Finns, including Törni's family in Viipuri, lost their homes and had to be resettled in Finland. This was approximately 10% of the entire Finnish population. 99% of the affected Finns refused to live under Soviet occupation, many having only 12 days to evacuate their homes. The ancient and beautiful city of Viipuri was virtually destroyed by Soviet artillery and some 11,600 bombs. The Törni family was forced to relocate to Vasa as refugees, and then to Helsinki where they live to this day. Years later, an author hauntingly wrote:

In the remote village of Uukuniemi, poised on the frontier with Russia, I visited a churchyard in which there were clusters of graves with the same family names. I could read from the birthdates inscribed that this was the burial ground of fathers, sons, brothers; of whole families wiped out in the 105 days from 1939 to 1940. There is no place so secluded as to have escaped the crimes of Josef Stalin.

The Winter War had ended but the Törni family suffered enormously. A grateful Finland awarded Sergeant Törni the Finnish Freedom Medals 1st and 2nd Class for his bravery during the Winter War. Returning to his regiment in May 1940 as a probationary Ensign, Törni continued to serve in the Finnish Army as an infantry platoon leader and training officer until May 1941. Still bitterly seeking revenge against his Soviet enemies, he watched as the Soviets once more made ever increasing demands upon the Finns and their sovereignty.

3

VOLUNTEER

Late in May 1941, Lieutenant Lauri Törni was called to the Infantry Regiment 12 (JR 12) headquarters. He had been serving as an infantry platoon leader and training officer since the end of his probationary period and had been preparing his new replacements for the fighting which he believed lay ahead. As an outstanding junior officer, LT Törni had once more come to the attention of his superior officers in the regiment. On that day, he was offered an opportunity which was to haunt him for the rest of his life, but one which he apparently never gave any serious thought to. He was asked if he would volunteer to attend a German Officer School in Germany. Törni lived for two things: Adventure and revenge against the Soviets. As one of his friends once related:

> *Törni as a young man loved adventure, danger,*
> *challenge, force, unpredictability and life-threaten-*
> *ing situations. He was a true hell-raiser. He lived*
> *for that and he did exactly what he wanted to do,*
> *especially when he was young.*

Seeing this as another opportunity for adventure, without hesitation, he eagerly volunteered to go to Germany with many other handpicked Finnish officers.

Törni, along with approximately 650 other selected Finnish Army officers and NCOs, arrived in Germany for training in late May or early June 1941 aboard the S.S. Bahia Laura. The Finnish Government, in an effort to modernize their army in the wake of weaknesses noted during the Winter War, lent officers to train with the German Wehrmacht. According to Professor Jukka Nevakivi, it was customary for Finland to send officers to Germany:

> *The Finnish independence struggle had, as a central player, the jaeger movement begun in 1915 when the Kaiser's Imperial Germany, in war with Russia, took on the training of a couple of thousand Finnish young men in its own jaeger battalions—Finland wanted independence even at the price of foreign arms.*

> *Secondly, the jaeger movement was renewed due to historical weakness in the spring of 1941 when the first participation of the Finns in the SS began. We wanted to train our men in the modern combat techniques even though the new jaegers returning from Germany would have brought the worst Nazi ideology into our army.*

As Lieutenant Colonel Lars Rönnquist, a former commander of Törni's related:

> *During the short Winter War Finland had suffered a considerable loss of officers, especially younger ones, and there was a need to make up for the loss. What happened in 1915, repeated itself in 1941: in 1915 Finland, then the Grand Duchy of the Tsarist*

Russia since 1809 was inspired by patriotism and sent in total secrecy about 2,000 young men to Germany to receive military training, with the objective to create a young and competent officer corps. In Spring 1941 similar, highly secret officer training was started for young volunteers in Germany which was then the only country where this type of training could be carried out. The project had no connection whatsoever with National Socialism or Nazi ideology but sprung from practical reasons.

Despite some initial political misgivings, Törni and the other Finns, with the official blessings of the Finnish government, sought to learn from the best soldiers in the world at that time. Unfortunately for Törni and the others, all foreigners trained in Germany were being trained by the elite Waffen SS. He and the other Finnish Army officers arrived for training at Stralsund, Germany. The Finnish officers were fitted for uniforms, issued their equipment and enthusiastically participated in the training.

Organized on 19 June 1941, Törni and the others originally wanted to call themselves the 'Jaegerbataillon' in honor of the 27th Jaeger Battalion which was formed of Finnish volunteers in 1915. However, the Germans initially gave the Finns the title, "Waffen SS Freiwillige Bataillon Nordost (Waffen SS Battalion Northeast)." Ignorant of the political implications, Törni proudly allowed himself to be photographed in his new Waffen SS uniform. Little did he know that his entrance into the Order of the Death's Head in 1941 as an Untersturmführer (2nd Lieutenant) and his swearing of "loyalty even after death" would haunt him years later.

Untersturmführer (2nd Lieutenant) Lauri A. Törni, Stralsund, Germany, June 1941. (Courtesy of Mrs. Kaija Mikkola).

The training curriculum was tough for the Finns, but they were a match for their German instructors. While the Waffen SS instructors wanted to impress their Finnish trainees with their own combat experiences and toughness, the Finns showed that they were equally experienced and tougher. In the end, it was the Waffen SS instructors who were impressed by Törni and the others. As the illustrious historian, Mr. John Keegan wrote in his book, *Waffen SS: The Asphalt Soldiers:*

> *A prototype legion was formed in May 1941 from a group of Finns, anxious to revenge themselves on Russia for the dictated peace of 1940, and their toughness and expertise augured well for the formation of others.*

The Waffen SS instructors imposed rigid, merciless discipline upon Törni and the other Finnish officer cadets from the moment that they met. Orders had to be obeyed immediately, without question and done correctly the first time. The phrase, "Zu Befehl!" (to be done), became an instinctive response to any order being given. Uniforms, boots, equipment, and weapons were given the best care and attention. Punishments were often given out and were swift and painful. The entire group was often punished for the error of one of the trainees.

Törni's easy manners initially got him in trouble, but he soon learned that nobody in the Waffen SS ever said thank you. Waffen SS soldiers and officers understood that they were given what they needed—no thanks were necessary. Törni's stay with the Waffen SS was unpleasant for both parties. His limited German, along with his quiet nature and reluctance to socialize with the Germans made him a sort of social outcast. Törni, like many Finns, viewed the Germans with the Finnish stereotype that they were an overrated and rather silly group of people. Meanwhile, the Waffen SS instructors drummed one fundamental principle into the Finnish cadets: The higher the rank, the more numerous the duties and the less the advantages. There were no separate dining facilities for the Waffen SS or their Finnish cadets; everyone ate and associated in the same area. If schnapps was available, the lowest ranks drank first and the officers/cadets got what was left which was often considerably less.

The Finns were taught that as leaders, they were expected to set the example and to ask their soldiers to perform only what they themselves were capable of performing. As such, the Finnish officer cadets underwent intense and very tough basic infantry training by their Waffen SS instructors who taught and led by example. Additionally, the Finns were taught that Waffen SS leaders led from the front where the phrase of "follow me" was more of a reality than a slogan.

In an almost fanatical manner, the Waffen SS instructors molded their Finnish officer cadets' bodies, minds, and spirits with the hope that their students would be physically and mentally prepared for the rigors of war. The training regimen, the balanced diet, and endless physical exertions kept the Finnish officer cadets in a continual state of fatigue. The Finns who survived the training were not the same men who had arrived. Emulating the examples of their Waffen SS instructors, they learned the virtue of hardships; renounced weakness and pity, sought sacrifice, exuded courage and displayed a rigid obedience. From the very first hour, the Waffen SS instructors ensured that the Finns didn't have much to eat, slept very little and were being made into machines only for commanding and killing. Weakness of any sort was not tolerated and those who showed weakness were sent packing. Fear, they were told, was their enemy.

Time and again, the Waffen SS instructors shouted that fear created weakness and that was the trainee's main enemy. The Finns understood that fear interfered with clear thinking at critical moments of battle and could kill them just as quickly as any unseen enemy. Törni and the others were continually challenged and tested to learn to control their fear. The brutal and exacting training had the desired effect. Törni, according to several soldiers who later served with him, was absolutely fearless in battle and never again thought about failure but would instead "will" his subordinates into performing seemingly incredible feats, while leading them through his own personal example.

A fighting spirit, the Waffen SS believed, could more than make up for a tactical or technical disadvantage. When in doubt of what to do, the Finns were urged by the Waffen SS instructors to attack. Aggressiveness was rewarded and encouraged. Törni responded and crossed the mental threshold to became a strong, courageous and ruthless being, without weakness, and who would never become corrupt.

During their training, the Finns were informed that Germany had invaded the Soviet Union on 21 June 1941 with the beginning of Operation Barbarossa. Although the Finnish government did not take part in the German invasion of the Soviet Union, Soviet air raids against Finland on 25 June 1941 gave the Finns the pretext that they needed. War was declared on the Soviet Union on 26 June 1941, and Finland appeared to be defending themselves against Soviet aggression. The Finnish Continuation War had begun. Finland requested that many of the officers training in Germany return home due to the hostilities.

In August 1941, after three intensive months, Törni and 19 other Finnish cadets completed their abbreviated training course and returned to Finland. It was said that Törni's departure was a relief for both Törni and his German instructors. Both seemed to have tolerated each other out of sheer necessity. Törni and many of the others were eager to return home and enter the new fight against the Russians. Fueled by revenge, they returned to Finland in August 1941 ready to use their new skills.

While Törni and the Finns were subjected to Nazi propaganda and theory during their training in Germany, they ignored it. The Finns probably did not understand the Nazi propaganda being offered since their German language skills were, for the most part, very basic and limited mainly to military situations rather than political concepts. The author has never found any evidence which suggests that Törni accepted the Nazi line.

As Lieutenant Colonel Rönnquist recently stated:

I knew Törni very well and can assure you that the Nazi movement and what it brought about never won his sympathy or mine. Our ultimate goal in all times was to retain the independence of Finland.

One of Törni's friends once stated:

It did not bother him if some political swill needed to be swallowed to get top-notch arms training for use against the Soviet Union, Stalin, Molotov and the Red Army. His aim was to defend the democratic system of Finland whatever the price. If you had to label him, I would say that he was a democrat with a small "d." Finns just cannot swallow theories of superior race because the Swedes at one time claimed that and the Czarists did too (i.e., The Czar was divine).

To the Finns, the political classes were only something which had to be endured as part of the overall training.

4

THE HUNTER

Törni and the other members of his Offizierschule class returned from Germany to once again find their homeland at war. The Winter War had left Törni and the other Finns with a feeling of injustice and uncompleted business. Germany had again begun to show an interest in Finland, and Finland entered into an uneasy agreement out of necessity rather than desire. Caught between the two great powers of Germany and the Soviet Union, Finland sought its own course while having to choose between the lesser of two known evils. The Soviet Union was openly hostile and imperialistic while Finland fearfully noted the occupation of the majority of Scandinavia by the Germans. Northern Finland soon became a German military area, occupied by the German Lapland Army, and an extension of German-controlled Norway.

Despite a common myth, Finland did not enter into an alliance with Germany; rather, Finland embarked in the Continuation War following a strategy which served Finland's own purposes. Finland had no interest in the ideology of National

Socialism and the Finnish government refused all ideological cooperation with the Germans. Fortunately for the Finns, Germany did not have sufficient military resources available at the time to force Finland's compliance with their wishes. Field Marshal Mannerheim accurately accessed the situation that Finland and the Soviet Union or Russia would still be neighbors after the war, regardless of the outcome. Due to the wise guidance of Field Marshall Mannerheim, Finland engaged in conflict against the Soviet Union with the intent of only regaining the territories lost during the Winter War, and not to participate in a struggle for conquest or domination as proposed by Germany.

Törni hurriedly reported to the 1st Finnish Division at Vieljärvi on the Karelian peninsula on 9 August 1941 where he met then-Captain (Cavalry) Lars Rönnquist. Captain Rönnquist was the commander of the 600-man mechanized Light Unit 8 (Kevytosasto - 8) which had been in heavy combat with the Soviets since mid-July 1941. Despite Finland's attempts to correct the deficiencies noted during the Winter War, the Finnish Army was still unprepared to fight a modern war. Lacking their own tanks, Rönnquist formed a small light armored unit of five captured Soviet tanks and armored cars and appointed Törni as the commander. Törni's light armored unit had two Vickers-type tanks, one Soviet T-28 tank and two armored cars which were fit for service. Despite having no training in armored warfare, the newly promoted First Lieutenant Törni and his new armored unit quickly entered into combat with the Red Army.

The fighting from July until December 1941 was fierce, particularly in Törni's sector just north of Lake Onega. The Finns, driven by revenge, tore into the Red Army making great advances against stiff resistance. Törni's armored unit conducted aggressive slashing attacks against the Soviets using the same roads which the Soviets had earlier built prior to the start of the Winter War. The Finns quickly regained most of the territory which they had lost to the Soviets during the Winter War and accomplished the majority of their military objectives by December 1941. Resisting German encouragement to continue their offensive and assist in the siege of Leningrad, the Finns continued to follow the guidance of Field Marshal Mannerheim and only sought to consolidate their gains. By January 1942, Finland had advanced as far as it would during the Continuation War, and entered into a static defense of its regained territories.

Törni remembered the Winter of 1942 as one of the most miserable of his life. Germany and Finland were in a marriage of convenience due to their common enemy, and Finland was now isolated from any possible assistance from the West. America and Britain had recently allied themselves with the Soviet Union against Germany, and had turned a blind eye to Finland's struggle. Soon, the winter darkness and intense cold once again settled upon the Finnish and Soviet combatants as both sides dug in for a long struggle. Until regular deliveries of German supplies arrived, Törni and the Finnish soldiers survived on the meager rations of only one cup of oatmeal, one pat of butter, and one piece of bread daily. But they fought on.

On 23 March 1942, Törni skied over a land mine while trying to capture some Russian prisoners. Wounded in the right thigh, right elbow, and bicep, Törni was evacuated and hospitalized. After convalescing in Vasa, Törni returned to the front where he was decorated with the Freedom Cross 3rd and 4th Class for valor.

Despite the handicap of having to learn as he went along, Törni was a very successful armor officer. Time and again, Törni's boldness and aggressive actions turned a decisive moment. Törni had seen extensive combat at Aanislina (Petroskoi, USSR), Karhumäki, and along the Stalin Canal (Povenets, USSR). However, due to the lack of spare parts, the armored unit was deactivated in July 1942 and Törni was transferred to the 56th Infantry Regiment (JR 56), lst Finnish Division, operating at Karhumäki. Reporting to the JR 56 headquarters, Törni was assigned as an infantry reconnaissance platoon leader.

Törni acted as an infantry reconnaissance platoon leader from approximately July until December 1942. During this time, both the Finnish and Soviet armies went into static defenses similar to the trench warfare of World War I. Being a small country, Finland was economically unable to maintain large numbers of soldiers under arms for an extended period. Therefore, whenever it was possible, Finland allowed soldiers to return to their homes to gather crops, etc. The Finns soon became seriously hindered and harassed by Soviet forces operating in their rear areas. Some of these units were left to operate as stay behind or partisan units as the Soviets retreated. Others were Soviet ski patrols which crossed the lines to conduct reconnaissance operations against the Finns. Finally, there were special Soviet units which parachuted behind Finnish lines to conduct sabotage operations.

Törni's unit was tasked to conduct counter-guerrilla and counter-reconnaissance operations against these various Soviet units. Acting in a manner similar to US Army Rangers, Törni and his men conducted operations lasting up to 10 or 11 days. These jaegers became the Finnish Army's answer to the Red Army marauders. Often unseen and unheard, Törni and his jaegers located the small Soviet bands and annihilated them. Ambush was the main tactic as the dense Finnish forests periodically reverberated with explosions and the rattle of small arms fire. It was a time when both sides paid little attention to the Geneva Conventions of War. Törni took great personal satisfaction in ruthlessly hunting down these Soviet units and annihilating them.

Finnish ski troop on patrol (Courtesy: Nils Lucander via John Larsen).

Young Finnish soldier on guard duty, August 1943, near Vonesentja (south of Lake Onega). Armed with Soumi submachine gun. (Courtesy: Nils Lucander via John Larsen).

By December 1942, Törni was appointed the commander of an independent jaeger company (Jääkärikompapania) and was tasked to conduct aggressive operations on both sides of the lines. Shortly thereafter, the Finnish jaegers swept into the Soviet rear areas where they slaughtered the Soviet support troops who erroneously believed they were safe from attack. Red Army headquarters, communications sites, and field kitchens were favorite targets. However, no target was safe from the roving Finns.

Sometimes, the jaegers engaged in sharp battles which degenerated into vicious hand-to-hand combat with bayonets, puukko knives, and small arms used as clubs. Despite their new reconnaissance and guerrilla operations behind Soviet lines, Törni and his jaegers still conducted anti-Soviet guerrilla operations behind Finnish lines where they continued to relentlessly hunt down and kill any Soviet infiltrators or reconnaissance parties found. Through these counter-guerrilla operations, the Finns kept the Red Army blind to their intentions. Törni's continued successes were soon noted with great interest by both the Finnish and Red Armies.

Majuri Lars Rönnquist was appointed Chief of the Operations Section of the lst Finnish Division in April 1943. Having heard of Törni's continued successes and his earlier favorable impressions of the young jaeger, Rönnquist ordered Törni to form a detached volunteer jaeger company (Jääkärit) for extended operations behind Soviet lines and to conduct anti-reconnaissance operations. Törni enthusiastically sought volunteers for his larger new command and was rewarded with some outstanding soldiers. Among them was a 20 year old Corporal Antti Lindholm-Ventola, one of his most steadfast men.

CPL Antti Lindholm-Ventola, 20 years old volunteer. Spring 1943. (Courtesy of Lindholm-Ventola family).

Private Mauno Koivisto, the future President of Finland, and his machine gun. (Courtesy of Petri Sarjanen).

The word was quickly put out throughout the 1st Division that volunteers were needed for a new special unit. Better rations, particularly chocolate, were a prime inducement for the volunteers. With practiced skill, Törni weeded out the Finnish volunteers who could not meet his demanding selection criteria. He sought out volunteers who displayed courage, physical endurance, initiative, resourcefulness, self-reliance, an aggressive spirit, and expert marksmanship. As was his habit throughout the Continuation War, Törni welcomed any and all volunteers, but swiftly rejected those who did not measure up. No shame was attached to their failure as those rejected were allowed to return to their parent units with no stigma attached. Corporal Lindholm-Ventola wrote a book about his experiences as one of Törni's jaegers entitled, *Lauri Törni ja hänen korporaalinsa (Lauri Törni and His Corporal)*. He related the following to the author before his death of cancer in February 1992:

I was one among the first ten men who had volunteered for duty with Törni, and whom he had selected for his new unit in 1943.

Törni's way of getting men to work for him was simple. He called all of the units within his division and asked for volunteers who would like to serve with him. When the time came for getting the selectees together at his command post, he himself called their organization's headquarters and named those he had selected. Thus, Törni got the cream of the volunteers.

It is a plain fact that without hard training and men with an excellent physical stamina, the end product, the achievements in combat would not be as good as they were. Upon the end of the war in 1944, there were only two men alive from the original men. I am the only one of those alive today.

What else could be said about Törni as a person? He took good care of his men, although he demanded a lot from everyone during training. Törni did not care too much about politeness; i.e., calling him 'Sir', etc. He was only 'Lasse' to everyone. "We will do it" was Törni's way of expressing a mission. There was never any whining or questions asked, not even during the situations when everyone was so tired that men began to fall asleep. His men had learned to take a nap even between combat actions. Törni was known as a tough fighter and killer. However, he was also a very sensitive person.

Begging, borrowing or stealing, Törni gathered all of the materials and equipment necessary for him to conduct the operations further behind Soviet lines where the jaegers knew that there was no hope of support from the Finnish Army. Törni passed along his combat lessons and techniques which he had learned from the Germans. Success in combat, he had learned, depended upon proper planning, good training, and luck. His jaegers were soon ready for the rigors ahead.

During one of his first operations with his new command, Törni and a squad of approximately 10 of his new jaegers were ordered to penetrate Soviet lines and ambush vehicles on a road about 12 miles behind Soviet lines. After surveying his maps and talking to Finnish intelligence personnel, Törni determined that the best way to attack the target was by small rowboats. His men rehearsed the mission over and over. Everything was relentlessly planned for, including the 35 lbs of equipment which each man carried in his pack.

The mission did not begin well—one of the men was too heavy and too rough while boarding one of the boats and crashed through the hull of the boat, sinking it. After doubling up, the now crowded boats were quietly rowed towards their Soviet targets. Törni's detachment left their boats hidden on the bank of the river and made their way to the ambush position by foot. Ambushes required patience and self-discipline. The Finns quietly set up their ambush position and waited for their prey to arrive. Törni and the Finns waited in ambush for so long that he considered canceling the mission. Finally, a single Soviet truck drove into the kill zone and the Finns launched their ambush.

The Soviet soldiers riding in the truck didn't have a chance. The Finns with their accurate rifle fire and fast firing Suomi submachine guns decimated the surprised Russians who offered feeble resistance. Törni and his men then rushed out in the kill zone to search the Soviet vehicle. Suddenly, another Soviet truck drove up and a brisk firefight ensued. The Finns closed with the arriving Russians and killed the majority of them before they could dismount from the truck. Another Soviet truck arrived and the fight degenerated into a close quarters battle. Rifles were swung like clubs, shots rang out at close range, puukko knives flashed, and even axes pried off of the trucks were used as killing tools. It was pure carnage as blood literally ran in rivulets from the trucks as the Törni and his jaegers butchered the Soviet soldiers. More and more Soviet soldiers arrived and joined in the fight. Desperately, Törni ordered his men to break contact and rendezvous in the safety of the dense forest believing that the Soviets were reluctant to follow the Finns into the forests.

Törni and his men were in a bind. Seeing what the Finns had done to their dead comrades, the surviving Red Army soldiers aggressively searched the forest looking for the raiders. Törni and his men quickly regrouped and made their way back to their boats. However, their escape route was blocked by Russian patrols. The entire sector was alive with Russian activity as they relentlessly searched for the bold Finns. Over the next several days the Finns evaded Russian patrols. Törni knew that time was of the essence and that he had to ensure that the intelligence he obtained got back to Finnish headquarters. He briefed each man so that if only just one survived, the Finnish headquarters would get the message. Törni's concern with returning with the information did not cause him to act recklessly. On at least one occasion, the Russians almost discovered the hiding Finns, but were killed silently with puukko knives. The Finns reached their boats and rowed to the safety of the Finnish lines. After spending 7 - 10 days behind Soviet lines, the Finnish jaegers returned to report to the lst Finnish Division headquarters.

Despite having only 11 men, it was estimated that Törni's jaegers had ambushed 300 Russians and killed over 100 of them without any casualties to themselves. What's more, the Finns were able to capture a Russian mailbag which contained plans and detailed information about the strengths and locations of the various Red Army units operating in the local area. This valuable information was put to use immediately by the Finnish lst Division. For Törni and his jaegers, this was the first success of many to come.

From the end of summer until December 1943, Törni and his small force of jaegers established and operated from a base camp deep behind Soviet lines. For a time, Törni operated the base camp and conducted combat operations approximately 80 miles behind the Soviet lines. At the time, it was not unusual for the jaegers to be ordered to ski 100 kilometers behind Soviet lines, hit a target and then return. Törni's jaegers primarily engaged in hit and run skirmishes, destroyed bridges; cratered and mined roadways, cut railroad lines, derailed trains, and destroyed ammunition and supply dumps. They boldly attacked enemy units, ambushed convoys, and cut communications.

Members of the unit told of Törni leading his men on search and destroy missions behind Soviet lines with the intent of killing every Soviet soldier they could find along the way. The marauding Finns struck terror in the Red Army which never knew when or from where the jaegers would attack. Törni frequently attacked a Red Army unit or target to get a reaction force to chase him. Using small Finnish anti-personnel land mines which are similar to the US Army M-14 "toe-poppers," Törni and his men hastily mined or booby-trapped their trail.

Often, the jaegers doubled back on their trail to ambush the Soviet pursuers. The results were predictable and devastating. The mines' explosive charges were small enough that when skied upon, the resulting explosion rarely killed, but maimed the Soviet soldiers. Another favorite Törni trick was to ski far behind Soviet lines and mine an area where the Soviets were known to operate. Törni enjoyed using the land mines as much for their psychological as well as their explosive effect.

Finnish ski patrol with reindeer. Reindeer were used to pull sleds and supplies. (Courtesy of Finnish Military Attache, Washington, D.C.).

Typical Finnish ski patrol. (Courtesy of Finnish Military Attache, Washington, D.C.).

Following his own interpretation of Lord Wellington's admonition that "the boldest course is often the safest," Törni attacked the Soviets with seemingly impunity. During one of the battles in the winter of 1943, Corporal Lindholm-Ventola described one of the more memorable actions:

> *I shall now tell you a combat story as an example of many of those battles which were fought during the winter of 1943. Our area of operations was 250 km wide. Our unit was deployed behind Lake Ontajarvi, within the enemy's territory, about 50 km behind the front lines. At one time a 200-man strong Russian ski patrol unit attacked us while we were conducting our normal search and kill missions within the enemy's own territory.*

Because our own strength was only 80 men, Törni decided not to attack or defend, but he decided to withdraw and mine our tracks and wait for a time to counteraction. The Russians continued their movement in columns of twos through our mine field. Our mines killed and wounded many of them. We lost three men killed in action and three wounded. This type of combat, so called delay-in-action with sudden two-sided attacks, was the type of combat they (the Russians) were afraid of.

Two of our killed men were placed into one ahkio (a boat-type of sleigh). It was very heavy to pull, even though the pullers were changed often. Was this a very sensible way to take care of our dead men while we, ourselves were in danger for getting wounded and, perhaps taken prisoners? We struggled hard with the enemy and had been skiing already for about 100 kms in the last hours. However, Törni's way of operation was always to bring the casualties into friendly lines, and thereafter to send them home. Whenever there was a possibility, one man from the unit attended the funeral and expressed condolences to the killed man's relatives. This was not a common practice in the Army.

It should be noted that Mr. Lindholm-Ventola related these stories to the author while he was painfully dying of cancer in 1992. According to his niece and others, Mr. Lindholm-Ventola was both pleased and proud that Americans were interested in the exploits of his commander and he thought that it was "important to him" to relay these stories before he died. With the same courage and dedication, Mr. Lindholm-Ventola displayed on the impossible missions against the Soviets, he ensured that he accomplished his final mission.

On several occasions, Törni's unit was almost disbanded, but each time Majuri Rönnquist listened to Törni's pleas for more firepower and volunteers. Törni was now allowed to expand his company to approximately 150 volunteers and to obtain more light machine guns and expert riflemen to be used as snipers. While the Finns preferred their Suomi submachine guns, Törni's men began to carry Soviet PPSH 41 and PPS 43 submachine guns along with DP 38 light machine guns. The use of the fast firing Soviet weapons created confusion in the Red Army during firefights and allowed Törni's men to use captured Soviet ammunition; thereby easing their resupply problems in the field.

The majority of the new volunteers came from Turku Province and were very clannish towards one another. These Finns were mainly from rural backgrounds, hardened by physical labor and quite comfortable living rough in nature. One of the most valuable volunteers, who was not from Turku Province, was Törni's new executive officer: Lieutenant Holger "Hoge" Pitkänen. LT Pitkänen had just completed his Officers Course when the Continuation War began. A buzzsaw of bravery, he had taken first place in tank destruction instruction during the Officers Course. Assigned to JR 56 as an infantry platoon leader, he was wounded just after the Finns had captured Petrozavodsk, the capitol of Soviet Karelia in late 1941. He returned to his unit after convalescing in the Spring of 1942. Just before volunteering for Törni's unit, LT Pitkänen had single-handedly captured several Soviet tanks. These captured tanks were immediately pressed into service by the Finnish Army, and LT Pitkänen jokingly complained that he would have won a medal if he had only destroyed them.

LT Pitkänen was an absolute wildman, and assisted Törni in whipping the expanded company into shape for combat. During this time, Pitkänen and Törni became close friends and often loaded each other's packs with 50 lbs of tiles before going off cross-country skiing together for up to 50 kilometers at a time. Physical fitness was expected from each and every volunteer upon arrival. To the consternation of many, the two officers often drank, wrestled, and sometimes fought together. They both shared an unquenchable love for adventure and had a sharp taste for combat.

One time in 1943, Lieutenants Törni and Pitkänen had removed their shirts and were sitting on the edge of a road sunbathing between operations. A Cavalry Colonel happened upon the two friends dozing in the warm sun and publicly harangued them for such unmilitary behavior. Awakened from his warm stupor, Törni allegedly grabbed the Colonel by the lapels and spread him across a car's hood. While choking and shaking the surprised Colonel like a wet dog, Törni said, "I am Lieutenant Törni of the Jaegers and I am ready to die for my country! Are you?" Törni then released the now frantic Colonel and shoved him away with contempt. Showing good sense, the Colonel straightened his uniform and hurried away without further comment while Törni went back to sunbathing with a laughing Hoge Pitkänen.

The idea of independent raiding forces was not uncommon in the Finnish Army or other armies at that time. The Finns formed "Sissibataliona" (Guerrilla battalions) to range behind Soviet lines in large unit strength. Since its formation, Törni's unit had operated under a variety of designations such as the Jääkärit, the 2nd Independent Company and 2nd Jaeger Patrol Company. These designations were frequently changed to confuse the Soviets. In a method similar to the British SAS, and to further confuse the Soviets, the volunteers were shown on military orders as "being on loan" from their parent regiments such as JR 56, etc. However, by December 1943, Törni's independent jaeger company was now known as the Osasto Törni (Törni's Unit). As was a common practice, the Finns named the unit after the commander. There were several units similar in size and mission as the Osasto

Törni, such as the Osasto Roininen, but none were ever as exceptional or as well known. Törni's men even took to wearing small triangular patches on their left sleeves to display their pride in belonging to the Osasto Törni. Their insignia was a sky blue cloth triangle with an embroidered stylized red letter "T" having a yellow lightning bolt crossing diagonally. The wearing of such insignia was unusual in the Finnish Army.

Through 1943 until early 1944, the Osasto Törni continued to wreak havoc on the Soviets while keeping their headquarters informed of the Soviets' movements. The company used every possible means to strike at the Soviet Army. Skiing, speed marching, hitching rides on trucks, swimming, using boats, and even riding bicycles, the Osasto Törni went immediately to where they were ordered. According to Pitkänen, the Red Army was rigid in its obedience to their orders and tactics. By their observations and reading captured Soviet manuals, Törni and Pitkänen knew beforehand moves and actions the Soviets planned.

The Red Army officers did not show much initiative and blindly continued on even when their plans had failed. Pitkänen said that because of this trait, it was easy to place land mines for the Soviets. The members of the Osasto Törni considered the Soviet soldiers like the Ukrainians as "harmless." Fresh Siberian soldiers who knew how to ski and were acclimatized to the harsh winter conditions were more of a threat. The Soviets, having had their nose bloodied by the Finns, learned the necessity of having hardy ski-troops inured to the hardships of winter warfare. Despite the Soviets continual improvement, the Finns continued to prove that they were superior ski-troops and soldiers.

By now, the Soviets had taken great interest in Törni and his jaegers. The NKVD (forerunners to the KGB) knew all about Törni and maintained a large dossier on him. The Finns soon began to encounter counter-reconnaissance forces composed of Finnish Communist expatriates; the most grudgingly respected group being commanded by a Major Valli. The Osasto Törni considered Valli's unit to be the most dangerous foe opposing them. Major Valli, ironically also from Turku, was a Finnish communist who escaped to the Soviet Union during the Civil War in 1918. Additionally, the Soviets offered a 3 Million Finn Marks ($500,000 present day dollars) bounty for Törni—dead or alive. Törni later wrote about the bounty:

> *The Russians dropped leaflets from planes and by radio, broadcast a reward of 3,000,000 Finn Marks was offered for my capture dead or alive.*

This bounty provided a great source of amusement to the members of the Osasto Törni who steadfastly admired their leader and didn't trust the Russians to honor their word even if they had shown treachery. Despite all of these threats, Törni and his jaegers soldiered on.

Except for some skirmishes and operations such as those conducted by Törni's jaegers, most of the Finnish-Soviet front became relatively quiet. Field Marshal Mannerheim quietly and uneasily discussed his concerns that the majority of the Finnish soldiers had forgotten how to fight—lulled into a dangerous complacency. His prophecy was all too true.

In June 1944, the Soviets opened a powerful offensive against the Finns along the Karelian Isthmus and the Lake Ladoga areas. On the second day, intense Soviet artillery barrages and massive infantry assaults punctured the Finnish defensive line. In one area, the Soviets fired their artillery at the rate of 400 rounds per minute on the Finnish positions. Red Army soldiers sometimes overran Finnish bunkers to find the Finnish defenders killed by explosive concussion. Some Finnish conscript units panicked and bolted from their fighting positions into the forests. Dogged Finnish veterans who held the line derisively joked that these panicked soldiers had joined the "Pine Cone Guards."

Finland's national survival once more hung by a thread; however, the Finns rose to the challenge by skillfully retreating more than 100 kilometers under fire while causing serious Soviet losses. The advancing Soviets found nothing of value in their path of advance as the Finns destroyed everything left in their wake. Emergency supplies of war materials, particularly the highly prized Panzerfaust anti-tank weapons, were rushed by the Germans to shore up the Finns. By July 1944, the Soviet advance was finally halted near the 1940 boundary lines. To the Soviets, Finland was merely a sideshow, while the Finns saw the offensive as an exhausting threat to their survival. Finnish leaders knew that diplomacy, not the force of arms, would save their sovereignty.

During the Soviet offensive, Törni 'willed' his jaegers to perform incredible feats of bravery well beyond their small numbers. At the beginning of the offensive, the Osasto Törni was operating with only 150 men. Within a month and a half after the Soviet offensive, the Osasto Törni's operational strength was down to 50 men.

According to Törni, the Osasto Törni had only just returned to their Finnish headquarters for a few hours after operating some 200 miles behind Soviet lines when the Soviet offensive erupted. Without a rest, they were hastily thrown into the line as the last reserves of the lst Division, even though they were not equipped to operate as regular line-infantry. It was a desperate time, calling for desperate measures.

To everyone's amazement, Törni and his jaegers counterattacked through the thick forests against the spearhead units of the Soviet advance with great success. The Finnish Battalion commander of the sector described Törni's boldness:

My plan was to provide Törni with some artillery and mortar support which would have probably delayed the start of his counterattack for about an hour. Lauri's plan was to attack immediately be-

fore the enemy would have a chance to dig in. I approved his plan. The counterattack in daylight through dense forest surprised the Russians and resulted not only in the destruction of an enemy battalion but also in saving a desperate situation.

Törni's jaegers remained mobile and moved from one hot spot to another which led the Soviets to erroneously believe that they were facing a force much larger than only about 150 Finnish jaegers. In the next week, the Osasto Törni went on the offensive against the Soviets twice more with great success. The small band of fierce jaegers inflicted tremendous losses, disrupted communications, and brought back desperately needed intelligence about the Soviet's activities. Day and night, they attacked the Soviets and only defended when circumstances dictated.

Finally, on 5-6 July 1944, the Osasto Törni was again committed to battle. The situation required them to stand or die, there were no other options. Led by their youthful iron-willed commander, the jaegers provided results well beyond their small numbers which had been depleted by the vicious and almost constant combat since June. Törni was ordered to hold a crucial crossroads near Ilomansti at all costs. The Finnish Army was falling back through the crossroads and was being relentlessly pursued by the advancing Soviets.

Törni, contrary to the usual rules of warfare, divided his small command and then shuttled back and forth between them while under heavy enemy fire. For the next two days of intense combat, the Osasto Törni, now less than 100 men, fooled the Soviets into believing that they were facing a much larger force, while the Finns inflicted heavy losses on the two Soviet regiments (approximately 4,000 men) facing them. Though lightly armed, the Osasto Törni held on by sheer fighting spirit—Törni setting the example for them to fight on despite their weariness. The strategic crossroads were held and the retreating Finnish army was saved by the Osasto Törni's

Lieutenant Lauri A. Törni, Knight of the Mannerheim Cross, August 1944. Award # 144. (Courtesy of LTC Raimo Vertanen, Foundation of the Knights of the Mannerheim Cross).

heroic actions. Once the danger had passed, Törni and his men broke contact with the Soviets and regrouped within the safety of the Finnish defensive lines. The heavy fighting was costly to the small band and the men were exhausted.

In late July or early August 1944, Törni was again wounded by a land mine explosion and was evacuated to a military hospital. The shrapnel injury to his forehead was Törni's third wound in his two wars against the Soviets. While convalescing, Törni learned that he was being made a Knight and awarded the Mannerheim Cross (Finland's highest award) for his actions at the crossroads near Ilomantsi. Additionally, on 27 August 1944, Törni was promoted to Captain while Lars Rönnquist was promoted to Lieutenant Colonel. Only a total of 191 Mannerheim Crosses have been awarded by Finland, and Törni was awarded #144.

According to the translation of Törni's official Mannerheim Cross award certificate:

The Commander-in-Chief has on this date 9 July 1944 nominated for: Freedom Cross, 2nd Class, and Mannerheim Cross Knight - Lieutenant Lauri Allan Törni.

Lieutenant Törni has performed throughout this war with Jaeger forces and as company commander in many battles, and in long distance patrol operations, as well as during the last year has demonstrated his own exemplary combat—2nd jaeger patrol commander's abilities. At the start of the enemy's powerful attack, Lieutenant Törni accomplished, with his company on 20 June 1944 a counterattack in which he destroyed many tens of enemy and held the enemy on a large front preventing it from accomplishing a threatened surroundment. On 24-26 June 1944 he cleared, on successful combat missions, the facing enemy forces and simulta-

neously his plans resulted in enemy losses. During 5-6 July 1944, Lieutenant Törni halted with his company, the advance of two enemy regiments, which already had succeeded in getting close to a certain road junction and were on the verge of cutting our forces' withdrawal. Nearly two days of continuous intense, maximum-severity combat saw him fully accomplish his task by causing the enemy the loss of hundreds of men and by preventing a threatening situation.

List of medals authorized by the Commander in Chief. No. 103/25-7-1944.

During the Winter and Continuation Wars, Törni won every medal for valor which Finland could bestow, as well as a German Iron Cross 2nd Class. The German Iron Cross 2nd Class was awarded to Törni in 1943. Although German and Finnish units fought against the Russians together, or the Germans had Finns assigned as scouts, there are no records to show that Törni ever fought alongside German units. LTC Rönnquist later explained that the Germans often gave the Finnish Army a draft of German medals to bestow on Finnish soldiers who were considered extremely valorous. Törni had been a recipient of one such medal. This awards practice was also common to Allied armies since the author's grandfather similarly won British and French medals for valor in combat during World War II.

5

WERWULF

On 19 September1944, the Finnish and Soviet Governments signed an armistice which ended the Continuation War. Far from capitulating, Finland had withstood a massive all-out Soviet offensive which was launched in June 1944 and had severely mauled the attacking Soviet forces; particularly at the final battle of Ilomansti. Finland and the Soviet Union had bludgeoned each other into a stalemate. Finland maintained its sovereignty, but had to return to the borders imposed back in 1940 at the end of the Winter War.

Thanks to the wise guidance of Field Marshal Mannerheim, who had advised against a war of conquest against the Soviet Union when the Continuation War began in 1941, Finland was momentarily spared from further retributions by the Soviet Union. With much of Finland in shambles and burdened with 480,000 refugees, General Mannerheim noted, "A high price had been paid for freedom. Fifty-five thousand white wooden crosses in our churchyards bear witness to that." Stalin soon redeployed the majority of his forces along the Finnish border and had them join in the final assault towards Berlin.

During this time, many high ranking officers in the Finnish Army did not trust that the Soviet Union would honor the armistice. They had seen Romania sign a similar accord with the Soviets only to be invaded by the Red Army. Recently, some Soviet units had crossed back into Finnish territory; the Red Army demanded that the Finnish Army return to its 1939 manning level of 41,000 men and further demanded the internment of the 200,000-man German Lapland Army still in Northern Finland.

The Finns had maintained cordial and cooperative relations with the Germans who began an orderly and slow retreat towards Norway. The Russians were not fooled, and threatened the Finns with invasion if the Germans were not expelled more forcefully. The German commander soon realized that the Finns could not resist Soviet pressure. After several incidents and German miscalculations, open warfare broke out between the Finns and the Germans. The Lapland War (1944 -1945) had begun as Finland turned against its former partner and the Germans resisted internment.

Fighting between the Germans and the Finns was intense. Both armies were well trained and hardened by the hostile environment of northern Finland. Bitter because the Finns had signed a separate peace with the Soviets and had ended their three year alliance, the Germans set fire to northern Finland. Instituting a scorched earth policy, the Germans did not limit their destruction to only targets of military value. Everything was deemed to be fair game. Whole villages were razed to the ground. Bridges were dropped, highways were rutted, harbors were blocked and power stations were destroyed. All together, more than 41,000 buildings were destroyed by the retreating Germans. A sign left by the Germans for the Finns bitterly stated, "Als Dank für <u>nicht</u> bewiesene

Wafenbruderschaft!"—"Thanks for nothing, comrades-in-arms!"

Special German engineering demolition squads were ordered to ensure that nothing left behind would be of value to the Finns or the Russians. Besides all of the wanton destruction, the Germans also left thousands of land mines in their wake which continued to kill Finnish civilians for many more years to come. So total was the destruction that five years of rebuilding was needed before the land was restored.

Meanwhile, a secret organization, the Asekätkenta (the Arms Hiders), was formed by Finnish patriots and plans were made to obtain the training, light weapons, ammunition, communications equipment, rations and clothing necessary to outfit a guerrilla force of 34 light battalions of 600-800 men, each ready to fight an underground war if the Soviets should invade. The members of the Asekätkenta were under no false illusions. They knew that the Finns could not halt a Soviet invasion, but they certainly intended to make the occupation a long and very costly affair. With alarm, they noted that Finnish Communists and sympathizers were coming out of hiding. They now feared a possible coup d'etat orchestrated by the Soviets.

As a provision of the Peace of Moscow, much of the Finnish Army was demobilized. Through Lieutenant Colonel Rönnquist, Captain Törni and his company requested a meeting with the 1st Division's Commander, Major General F.U. Fagernäs, and volunteer for combat in the north against the German Lapland Army. General Fagernäs refused the request citing the recent losses suffered by Törni's battalion and the fact that the 1st Division was not destined to be part of the special army corps being sent to fight the Germans. Among the staff officers, it was quietly agreed that Törni had seen too much killing and needed a rest. The General's decision was bitterly accepted by Törni who was determined to fight **any** invader on Finnish soil.

On 11 November 1944, Captain Lauri Törni was discharged from active duty. For the first time in his life, the 25 year old, newly-promoted Captain, Knight of the Mannerheim Cross and national hero, was without a job and without any future prospects. Bitter and still seeking revenge against the Soviets and Communists whom he obsessively hated, Törni thought about the loss of his beloved home town of Viipuri which was now occupied, the deaths of his many friends, and his personal struggle against the Russians which began so many years before.

Returning to his family in Helsinki, Törni had more to brood about. Communist sympathizers infiltrated the government and the police. Always somewhat naive about political matters, Törni sought to continue with his life as a civilian in the belief that somehow all would be forgiven and forgotten. Shedding his uniform, Törni went in search of work. But his job applications were rejected or ignored. Time and again, Törni's requests for a job were denied for he was a man to be feared due to his previous officer training in Germany by the Waffen SS. The politics of the time made him a marked man; he was now branded as a Nazi and avoided. As one of his friends noted, "he had the Mark of Cain."

Former members of the Asekätkenta told the author that Törni was not a member of their underground group, and the author has not seen any records to suggest otherwise. Still, Törni later claimed that he was approached by two Finns who were active in the Asekätkenta and was quietly asked to participate. These Finns offered him a chance to do his "desired work," asked him to travel to Germany for special training; obtain all of the weapons and explosives that he could, and then teach what he had learned to the Asekätkenta upon his return. On 21 January 1945, Lauri Törni again bid his family farewell, and made his way to Vasa, Finland where he secretly boarded a German U-Boat and travelled to Germany.

Just prior to his departure from Finland, Törni assumed the name of **Lauri Laine** to disguise the fact that he was again involved with the Germans. Aboard the U-Boat, Törni (Laine) met a retired Finnish officer, Solmu Korpela, and ten other Finns also on their way to Germany for specialized training. Arriving in Schweinemund, Germany in February 1945, Laine and the other Finns travelled to Neustrelitz, Germany. Törni had told his friends after the war that he had received special training at Mecklenburg; however, the author has seen documents and statements from Törni which confirm that he attended special training at Neustrelitz. Laine and the other Finns had been sent to attend the Guerrilla Warfare and Sabotage Course hosted by the Waffen SS as part of the Werwulf Organization.

Originally organized by Major General Gehlen as spy and radio networks, the responsibility for the Werwulf Organization was transferred to Reichsführer Himmler. However, Gehlen kept an active interest. The planning for the Werewolves has been variously attributed to Reichsführer Himmler, SS General Kaltenbrunner, SS General von dem Bache, SS Lieutenant General Pflaume, and Major General Gehlen. Both Generals von dem Bache and Pflaume had extensive experience fighting the French Underground.

The Werwulf Organization was formed to provide special training to selected German soldiers who were then expected to conduct guerrilla operations against the occupying Allied forces; a threat which the Allies took seriously. The Allies expected a guerrilla campaign to be waged against them for up to two years after the defeat of Germany. However, as Gehlen saw it, all Werwulf operations were to be directed exclusively against the Russians. Nothing in his plan concerned underground resistance against the Americans, British or French.

While some believed that the Werewolves were formed to guard Hitler's Alpine Redoubt in Southern Germany, Gehlen actually planned his formations in a more conventional manner. He believed that the Western and Soviet alliance would not last long after the defeat of Germany. Rather, he envisioned a partisan organization, fighting against the Russians which would finally be embraced by the Western Allies. As Gehlen saw it, once the Western Allies learned the true meaning of Stalin and the Communists, they would unite themselves with the defeated Germany and fight together to liberate Europe from Bolshevism.

The title for the Werewolves came from the German Propaganda Minister Dr. Joseph Goebbels' fertile mind and was based upon German Middle Ages folklore. According to legend, werewolves were men capable of transforming themselves into ravenous wolves having the powers of the Devil and were invulnerable except to weapons consecrated by the patron saint of hunters, St. Hubertus. The Nazis loved the romantic image of the werewolves and incorporated the legends into the Hitler Youth indoctrination training program.

Frequent radio broadcasts by Dr. Joseph Goebbels exhorted the volunteers to ruthlessly deal with anyone who attempted to conquer Germany. One such broadcast stated, "We Werewolves consider it our supreme duty and right to kill, to kill, to kill, employing every cunning and wile in the darkness of the night, crawling, groping through towns and villages, like wolves, noiselessly, mysteriously..." Still another broadcast urged the Germans that they, "Must defend ourselves and our loved ones, bravely and secretly. We must creep up like footpads, destroy and get rid of the communist rabble which is ravaging our Fatherland..."

Those selected for Werwulf training were sworn to absolute secrecy and any breaches of security were dealt with swiftly and harshly, sometimes even by murder. SS Obergruppenführer Hans Prutzmann was appointed as the commander. Experienced in fighting the Soviet partisans, Prutzmann was well known for his ruthless severity. Werwulf formations were originally based upon the organization of the Nazi Party clandestine cells of the 1930s; Dorfortsgruppe (village groups), GemeindeOrtsgruppe (rural district groups), and Stadtsgruppe (town groups), etc. Local German army commanders located where Werwulf operations were scheduled were requested to provide arms, ammunition, explosives, and rations but this rarely occurred.

Gehlen, impressed by his review of Polish General Bor-Komorowski's organization of the Polish Underground Army which was recently defeated in Warsaw, incorporated many of the Pole's ideas into Werwulf training and clandestine organization. A variety of special training was provided by the Waffen SS instructors who had learned their hard lessons in guerrilla warfare from the various underground and partisan groups which they had fought from France to the Soviet Union. With the support of German Intelligence, the Waffen SS instructors:

a) Trained saboteurs and guerrilla fighters.

b) Formed action units of no more than 60 men each.

c) Taught the preservation of salvaged arms and their safekeeping at secret hideouts.

d) Taught the setting up of secret radio posts and communication nets.

e) Taught espionage within the Soviet military command and occupation authorities.

f) Formed 'liquidation commandos' against Soviet military leaders and officials in occupied territories.

g) Taught the preparation and dissemination of anti-Soviet propaganda by underground press, leaflets, radio, and by word of mouth.

Werwulf volunteers were selected for their enthusiasm, willingness, doggedness, toughness, and ingenuity. Being good soldiers was desirable, but not deemed to be entirely necessary since the instructors were tasked to fill in any gaps in training. The following criteria was used to select basic Werwulf candidates:

The guerrilla must be an excellent soldier and unite the capabilities of an infantryman with those of an engineer. Furthermore, his mission requires from him a close relationship to nature, frugality and ingenuity in the exploitation of all means and makeshifts available. Through his behavior towards the population, he must win the confidence and respect of all freedom-loving people. Weaklings and traitors must fear him like the plague.

As future guerrilla leaders, Laine and the other Werewolves were selected due to the following criteria:

The leader of a guerrilla unit should be demanding of himself and others, while conducting his mission. On the other hand, he must provide never-ending concern for the welfare of his men, thus maintaining the battle-worthiness of his unit.

His daring as a combatant, his leadership success and his unconditional fairness must waken confidence. Confidence is the fundamental of leadership in guerrilla units.

The authority of the leader rests solely on his personality, not on rank and insignia.

The leader of a guerrilla unit carries a high measure of responsibility. He has the same rights as the commander of an independently operating battleship, and he may impose any punishment—even death—to keep up discipline.

Laine, again naive to the political implications, characteristically dove into his new training with boundless enthusiasm. In the following weeks, the Finns and other volunteers learned the German concept of the fundamentals of guerrilla warfare, guerrilla intelligence, weapons, tactics, and sabotage through the use of chemicals and explosives. Special emphasis was given to the destruction of Soviet tanks, particularly with the Panzerfaust anti-tank weapon and explosive satchel charges. Additionally, the Finns were taught clandestine recognition signals, rudimentary espionage tradecraft, secret passwords, and how to deal swiftly and ruthlessly with traitors and collaborators. Each was taught to recognize the "Wolfsangel," the runic letter which was to be painted on buildings occupied by the foreign intruders and on the houses of German traitors, collaborating with the "occupiers," marking them for destruction by explosives and arson.

Laine watched as defeatism hindered the formation of Werwulf combat units. Formations of Hitler Youths, some as young as nine years old were press-ganged into combat service in defense of the Reich. The quest for vengeance and a fear of Soviet atrocities were burned into the souls of these children. Fanaticism glowed like a fever from their young eyes as they truly believed that they were somehow the saviors of Germany. Their Fuhrer had told them so, and like the Japanese Kamikazes, they were prepared to sacrifice themselves for the Fuhrer and the Fatherland.

NOTE: Although deserted by their officers, some Werwulf groups conducted limited and isolated operations against Western and Soviet forces. Only a few weeks after the end of the war, youthful Werewolves performed sabotage and murder against British units. In one case 13 youthful, self-admitted and unrepentant Werewolves were tried, found guilty by a military tribunal, and executed for their underground activities. In December 1945, the US Army Counterintelligence Corps crippled Werwulf activities in the American Zone of Occupation by arresting approximately 800 Werwulf members during a massive roundup. Two Werwulf leaders were arrested in 1946 and received prison terms for attempting to reactivate their Werwulf cells in Frankfurt. Arrests of Werwulf leaders continued until as late as 1960 as they attempted to reactivate their underground cells. Many former Werwulf members are still involved in German right-wing political parties and groups. The only activities which were moderately successful, and to which Gehlen gave any serious consideration towards, were the clandestine Werwulf cells, sabotage groups, and radio posts in East Prussia, Pomerania, Silesia and Poland. Gehlen made use of some of these groups in later years when he was involved with the West German Intelligence service (Org, later the BND).

With the rapid approach of the Red Army from the east, the sabotage course was prematurely curtailed in March 1945. Laine and the ten other Finns were sent by the Germans to Heringsdorf, Germany to await their transportation back to Finland. Waiting in Heringsdorf for approximately one month, the other Finns passed the time learning Morse Code and radio communications from the Germans, but Laine showed absolutely no inclination to learn such things. Laine passed the time by exercising and dreaming of fighting the Russians once more. By April 1945, the Finns were again moved to Flensburg, Germany to escape the advancing Russians.

After two more weeks of waiting in Flensburg, the Germans informed the Finns that they were unable to provide transport back to Finland. There were no ships available; the Finns were now stranded in Germany. Impatient, Laine then requested the local German commander for permission to join the other German forces on the front line and fight the Russians. He reasoned that if he could not return home to fight the Russians, he could stay in Germany and still fight the Russians. At first, Laine's request was denied.

Meanwhile, in Finland, the dreaded Finnish State Police (Valpo) had discovered some of Asekätkenta's hidden weapons and supplies. The Finnish Communists tried to excuse their treason by stating that had they not done so, the Soviets would have invaded. In reality, these Finns received their orders from Moscow. Informants and opportunists often betrayed their friends and neighbors. Some 2,000 leaders of the Asekätkenta were arrested and imprisoned as traitors while others were barely able to flee to nearby Sweden. For some, a panicked whispered word on the telephone saved their lives and allowed them to escape just moments ahead of their captors. Trust was a rare commodity.

The Valpo's ruthless searches and actions led to an atmosphere of fear and insecurity throughout Finland as the Finnish patriots were rounded up and imprisoned. Through fear and intimidation, the members of the Asekätkenta were now viewed as traitors rather than the patriots they were. As in the Soviet Union, opposition was tolerated and was ruthlessly dealt with.

With Marshal Rokossovskii's Second Belorussian Front rapidly advancing westward across northern Germany, Laine and the other Finns faced a choice which they did not linger upon. Laine was a Finnish National, in Germany, attending a German school, had been trained by the Waffen SS and well known to the Red Army due to his exploits during the Continuation War.

Once more, he approached the local German commander and asked for permission to go to the front lines and fight the Russians. The German commander relented and finally allowed Laine, Korpela, and a third Finn to join a 200-300 man provisional German Marine battalion preparing to leave for the front lines. Laine accepted a commission as a German officer, allegedly holding the honorary rank of Hauptsturmführer (Captain), and was placed in charge of the German Marines. With arms, supplies, and ammunition soon distributed, Laine led his new ragged command into combat against the Russians near Schwerin, Germany. It was a familiar task, and he was more than prepared for the challenge.

Laine, the other Finns, and the German Marines arrived in Schwerin just in time to see the German Army collapse before the Red Army in full retreat. Hysteria and chaos ruled the battlefield as the Germans' fighting spirit broke. With a total lack of organization, Laine's unit joined the retreat and fought a series of vicious skirmishes with the advancing Red Army. As he surveyed his unit, Laine saw a mixture of old men and young boys who had been thrown together and expected to perform miracles. Despite his limited German language abilities, his Marines had seen him in combat and he had their confidence while he attempted to keep them together as a cohesive fighting unit. Their survival depended upon this, and they trusted Laine.

He knew that their salvation lay to the West where they would fare better if they could surrender to the Allies rather than the Russians. Laine, and the other Finns knew that there could never be any surrender to the Soviets for them. Over the next few weeks, Laine's troops avoided the Russians whenever possible and fought only when forced to do so as they moved westward towards the Allies. Allied fighter-bomber aircraft bombed and strafed them without warning, shooting up anything that moved. Sometimes, Laine's German Marines would suddenly run into a Soviet tank column which had somehow raced ahead of the main forces, unhindered by air attacks. Whenever feasible, the Germans would break contact and avoid fighting as they continued to move west. However, whenever they were forced to fight, Laine and his Marines gave a spirited account for themselves. All of his skill, daring, and leadership was needed to survive.

V-E Day, 8 May 1945, found Laine and the remnants of his hardy band surrounded and far behind Russians lines near an airfield on the outskirts of Hagenow, Germany. Just north of the Elbe River, they were still within the Soviet Zone of Occupation. The Russians kept the German perimeter under artillery fire and periodic assaults. One by one, the German Marines watched as other nearby German pockets of resistance were crushed beneath the treads of the Soviet armor. Desperate to find any salvation for his soldiers, Laine fought his way out of the Russian encirclement and made contact with elements of the American 17th Airborne Division at the Hagenow airfield sometime around 11 May 1945. Surrendering to the Americans, he was amazed to find that the Americans gave him ammunition and supplies and advised him to have his unit continue fighting the Russians, "As long as you can to get your people out."

Laine rejoined his unit and together they fought their way out of the Russian encirclement as the Americans had advised. It took another day of hard fighting for all of the Germans and Finnish stragglers to finally reach the American lines. Stacking their arms, Laine formally surrendered his German Marines to the American paratroopers who were assigned to support the British 2nd Army. But the Russians were fully aware of what was going on and soon demanded that the Americans turn over all of the captured Germans and Finns to them insisting that they were their prisoners.

To their credit, and to Törni's eternal gratitude, the tough American paratroopers refused to surrender the now defenseless German prisoners and aggressively protected them from Russian retribution. Operating north of the Elbe River, the Americans were ordered to pull back to positions south of the Elbe River. The Russians menacingly brandished their weapons, surrounded the American vehicles and then told the Americans that they would not be allowed to pull back across the Elbe River, to which the Americans replied, "Try and stop us!" With that, the Americans and their German prisoners convoyed back across the Elbe River to their headquarters while the Russians stood by and did nothing to halt them. In a sense,

Major General Gehlen's prophecy of the split between the Soviets and the Allies was starting to come true. Unknown to anyone at the time, the Cold War had just begun as the Allies began to turn on one another.

6

THE BEGINNING OF A
NEW LIFE

Törni, the Finns and his German Marines were now safe from the Russians. He had survived three wars in six years, but the end of these conflicts had brought new situations which would lead to unforeseen challenges and dangers. He began a nine-year period in which he rarely spoke except to his closest friends.

Although captured by the American 17th Airborne Division, technically Törni (still known as **Lauri Laine**) was captured in the British Zone of Occupation as agreed to at the Allies' Yalta Conference. Because of this geopolitical decision between the Allies, Laine and the other prisoners were turned over by the Americans after about a week to the British Army for internment. This seemingly insignificant act would have larger consequences in Törni's life months later.

Had Törni actually surrendered or been captured prior to 8 May 1945, he would have been classified as a Prisoner of War (POW) and would have been theoretically protected by the Geneva Conventions. Because Törni surrendered to the Americans after 8 May 1945, he was considered "Disarmed Enemy Forces" (DEF) by the Americans and a "Surrendered Enemy Personnel" (SEP) by the British. DEFs or SEPs were not considered protected by the Geneva Conventions by either the Americans or the British. Törni's fate now depended solely upon the good graces of his captors.

Despite his new status as a SEP, and the fact that he had been a Finnish National serving in the Wehrmacht, Laine was quite fortunate to have been interned by the British. The DEFs were sometimes treated harshly by the Americans. While the Americans certainly had little love for their former enemies, most of the American soldiers were more concerned about going home than the welfare of their German prisoners. Laine was fortunate not to have been a prisoner of the French who were extremely vindictive towards their German captives. Motivated by embarrassment and revenge, the French used their German prisoners as slave labor. The ranks of the French Foreign Legion swelled with German "volunteers" who sought to escape the hardships of internment. Many Germans died in Indochina and other former French colonies as the French sought to reestablish their empire after the war.

The British Army alone had over 2 million German POWs and SEPs in captivity by 8 May 1945. Laine was thrown into this situation, and as always, made the best with what he could. He, his fellow Finns, and the other Germans were marched westward for another three weeks into British captivity near Lübeck, Germany, arriving there in late May or early June 1945.

Although the British were much more relaxed in their treatment of the German prisoners than the Americans, and certainly the French, there was a shortage of food, water, sanitation, and shelter at Lübeck. Dehydrated, hungry and severely fatigued from his march into captivity, Törni arrived at Lübeck to be greeted by the sight of a bleak outdoor prison camp filled with German POWs who were walking skeletons, half naked, filthy; with long matted hair and beards, whose skin was leather brown from the exposure to the elements, and all suffering from malnutrition. The British attempted to provide tents, but there were so many Germans that the prisoners simply dug holes and lived in the earth as animals. For months, these Germans had lived and slept in the shallow holes. The wind stirred up the dust into a low-lying haze, while each rain turned the barren land into a sea of mud.

Winter loomed ominously in the future and the food stockpiles were controlled by the Americans. So desperate was the food situation in Europe in 1945 that General Montgomery, commander of all British forces in Europe, had to order all British and Canadian forces to cease looting and foraging the countryside for food. At Lübeck, as in all of the Prisoner of War camps, each prisoner did what was necessary to survive. The strong survived and the weak perished. Friendships and loyalties vanished in the reality of survival. There were frequent riots as some prisoners tried to distance themselves from the Germans by claiming to be foreigners who had been pressed into German military service.

Feeding time was a frenzy of fists and boots as everyone attempted to get their share of the food and water. Hunger was a constant and ruthless companion. Prisoners traded everything in order to get enough to eat, even the belongings and gold teeth of the dead. Cigarettes could buy anything. Anarchy reigned as informers, fanatics, cowards, madmen, and thieves circulated through the camp. While most prisoners were resigned to their fate, some prisoners like Törni sought escape and freedom at any price. Törni surveyed the scene around him with disdain. The once proud and arrogant Germans who had conquered most of Europe were now reduced to simple, underfed men standing in the rain waiting to be fed by their conquerors.

Within days of his arrival at Lübeck, Törni and the other newly arrived prisoners were put into long lines awaiting a health inspection. After that, the prisoners were placed in long lines waiting to be interrogated by control and verification teams. As he moved closer and closer to the building, fear began to grow in Törni's stomach. Finally, he entered the building and found himself standing in front of a table behind which sat various British and Canadian soldiers. Left standing, Törni was questioned. What's your name? Where were you born? Where is your paybook? What was your last unit? Where did you surrender to Allied forces? When did you surrender? The questions seemed to go on forever. Finally, he was told to return to the main prisoner compound. Törni was terrified of the unknown. There were unsubstantiated rumors that the British and Americans were turning over certain prisoners to the Russians. "Surely this can't be," thought Törni and the other Finns.

Törni decided to escape from the camp but the exact situation of his escape or release from the British is not known. There are several different versions. Törni had a habit of telling different versions of his life to people. Only his closest friends know of the truth about what actually occurred throughout his life, and each of them have a slightly different slant. One version is that Törni was spotted by British Intelligence as being wanted by the Soviets. Another version is that an informer told the British about his past. Törni was certainly wanted by the Soviets because of his war record during the Continuation War. Also, Törni had been trained by the Waffen SS. Because of his association with the Waffen SS, Törni knew that none of the Allies would be sympathetic to his situation. The British were part of a commission charged with the occupation of Finland after World War II and were therefore in close coordination with the Soviets. When requested, the Allies often gave German POWs to the Soviets, and even General Eisenhower had signed orders for the forcible repatriation of former Soviet POWs back to the Red Army. This despite Stalin's open boast about wanting to shoot thousands of German POWs after the war. Törni later denied that he had been processed or interrogated by the British and there is no record of him ever being held as a prisoner by the British. Perhaps Törni escaped because he had been identified. Perhaps he simply decided not to become another statistic or skeleton dying of hunger. Perhaps he had been released due to the relaxed British "De-Nazification" program. The British had over 2 million prisoners in May 1945, but were down to approximately 68,000 in the spring of 1946. Törni was confident in his ability to escape and survive and began his journey home to Finland sometime in July 1945. According to Törni, after about a month of being held at Lübeck, he and Korpela simply walked away from the camp. In the absolute confusion and wreckage of Europe in 1945, Törni and Korpela began to walk towards Kiel, Germany while subsiding on what they could buy, beg or steal and sleeping wherever and whenever they could. They became faceless members of the millions of homeless Europeans trying to get home after the war. Just north of Kiel, Törni and Körpela decided to boldly try hitchhiking a ride to Flensburg.

A British Army captain stopped his jeep and gave the two Finns a ride. Amazingly, the Finns learned that the captain was the commanding officer in Flensburg and was more than happy to give them a lift. Törni and Körpela lied to the captain telling him that they had been prisoners of war of the Germans and that they were trying to get home to Finland.

Arriving in Flensburg, the British officer directed them to the Swedish Consulate. They were then informed that the Danish border and ports were closed, but they might open in a few days. The two Finns remained in Flensburg for approximately three weeks, but their restlessness to get home caused them to take risks and cross the border into Denmark. Leaving Flensburg, Lauri Törni again changed his name. This time, he took the name of **Aulis Haapalainen**. Törni had met Haapalainen earlier in training at Neustrelitz and had learned that he had been captured by the Germans in 1944 during the

83

Lapland War. Therefore, reasoned Törni, by assuming Haapalainen's identity, he could safely claim that he had been a German prisoner of war. While the real Haapalainen remained in Flensburg, Korpela and Törni then sneaked across the Danish border at night dressed in civilian clothes that they had somehow obtained.

Safely across the border, they again went to the Swedish Consulate, this time at Aabenraa, Denmark. The two Finns boldly told the Swedes all their tales of woe and the Swedes then contacted the Danish authorities who provided the wily pair with transport to Copenhagen. Arriving in Copenhagen, Haapalainen (Törni) and Körpela made their way to the Finnish Consulate where they obtained the necessary papers to return home to Finland.

After the short voyage across the Baltic Sea, along with a short stop in Sweden, Törni arrived in Turku, Finland in August 1945. But Finland had drastically changed and even more dangers and challenges awaited him upon his return.

7

INNOCENT

Törni now entered the "lost period" of his life. Only his closest friends knew of his adventures during this time. One friend, Colonel Paavo Kairinen had been a member of the Asenkätkenta and had fled to the United States. Colonel Kairinen's and Törni's lives would intersect many times in the future, as Colonel Kairinen would write in his excellent book, *Marttisen Miehet, Asekätkijäveljet (Marttinen's Men - The Brotherhood of Armaments Concealers)*.

Törni could barely conceal his excitement as the ship carrying him home from the wreckage of Germany entered Turku harbor. He had made it. He had survived the war and the resulting captivity and was able to see his native land. Törni once again believed that all was well in the world and was unaware of the reign of terror being conducted by the Valpo.

Leaving the ship and starting home on foot towards Helsinki, Törni was soon stopped and questioned about why he did not have any identification papers or documentation. Believing that he had nothing to hide, Törni gave his real name, rather than Haapalainen's, only to find himself being arrested by the feared Valpo. Confused by his arrest, he was informed that he was considered a traitor to Finland and would be detained at the dreaded Hanko Prison. Törni knew that only the worst criminal offenders went to Hanko Prison. Escape from Hanko Prison was virtually imposible. Offering no resistance, Törni was placed on a train heading towards Helsinki and Hanko Cape. Realizing once more that the safest course is often the boldest, he quickly developed a plan and escaped from his Valpo guards during a train stop at Karjaalla.

His escape plan succeeded and he was soon in Helsinki reunited with his family. They warned him to be careful, but he was determined to lead a normal life as an average citizen. Törni openly sought work. After all, he mistakenly reasoned, he had done nothing wrong, and there was no shame in his past. Finding employment in an electrical supply house, he led a fairly normal life in Helsinki near his parent's home until February 1946 when he was betrayed to the Valpo by an informant co-worker.

During the year of 1946, Finnish newspapers printed daily stories regarding treason and the dangers of Fascism. Törni's picture, along with several other Finnish officers accused of being Fascists frequently accompanied and illustrated these lurid jaunts of journalism. And so, in October 1946, the "Great Treason Trial" began in the district court of Turku. The trial was a sham with the sentence already determined despite the evidence, or the lack of it. Brought before the court as a nameless prisoner bound in shackles, Captain Lauri Allan Törni, was publicly branded as a traitor to Finland and sentenced to six years in prison to be followed by another four years of probation. It was a severe sentence, and one which Törni did not understand or deserve. He was stunned, unable to comprehend what was occurring. After all, he had only done his duty as a Finnish officer.

Quickly transported to the Turku State Prison, Törni began to serve his sentence, but secretly planned another escape. The thoughts of escape were constantly on his mind, but he patiently waited for the right moment. With the help of a trusted friend, Törni's moment arrived in the spring of 1947 when he was able to obtain an illegal identification card and literally walk out of the prison as another man. Quickly contacting his friends, Törni continually stayed on the move, always one step ahead of the Valpo. According to what Törni later told Colonel Kairinen, the State Police knew Törni all too well and began broadcasting stories across Finland about how the national hero was really a thief. As expected, this was too much for an honest man to bear and Törni turned himself in to the police in Oulu. Secured with handcuffs and shackles, Törni was returned to the Turku State Prison. He would ultimately serve his sentence in prisons in Helsinki, Turku, and Riihinaki, Finland.

As is common throughout Törni's life, there is a second story about his escape from the Turku State Prison in the Spring of 1947. Once he had escaped, he contacted his old friend, Holger Pitkänen. They somehow learned that there was an escape route from Finland to Sweden through the northern Finnish town of Törnio. Pitkänen's sister was a war widow attending the Teacher's Training College in Törnio on a scholarship. Törnio was her late husband's home town, so she was well known in the area and could ask questions without raising suspicions. On the day of their arrival, Törni and Pitkänen were dismayed to learn that a Finnish family had been shot down on the ice of the frozen river while trying to cross over to Sweden.

Despite their concern, Pitkänen and his sister went on a reconnaissance trip across the border to Haparanda, Sweden the day after their arrival. The custom's officials were locals and friends of Pitkänen's late brother-in-law, and were therefore not suspicious when his sister explained that she wanted to show her brother the sights from the Swedish side of the border. Once on the Swedish side, one of the border guards, who was ethnically Finnish and bilingual, told Pitkänen, "If you manage to come here, inside my office, I'll give you the stamp." Pitkänen and his sister quickly returned to Törnio and met Törni who was waiting in a local hotel. Pitkänen explained his plan to Törni that evening.

The next morning, Törni and Pitkänen hailed an unsuspecting taxi and put their plan into action. According to Pitkänen, he waved a large bunch of money in the driver's face while Törni pointed a pistol at the driver's back. The driver was told: "Drive to the Lantfiskal's office in Haparanda and you get the money or else..." Knowing that the Lantfiskal's office was only 100 - 200 meters across the border, the driver took the risk and sped through the border checkpoints. Stopping hard in front of the Lantfiskal's office in Haparanda, Sweden, the driver got his money as Törni and Pitkänen rushed inside. The pursuing Finnish Customs agents were too late to do anything since Törni and Pitkänen's visas had been quickly approved and stamped as promised. Leaving the Lantfiskal's office, the two friends loudly laughed at the Finnish Customs agents as they calmly strolled to a nearby train station and purchased tickets for the next train to Stockholm.

Arriving in Stockholm, the two Finns met their contact, a dowager countess of a castle near the town of Sigtuna, Sweden. Over a pleasant lunch, the dowager told Törni and Pitkänen to continue traveling to the 17th Century castle at Skokloster, Sweden where she would meet them in a couple of days after she took care of some business.

Pitkänen and Törni arrived at Skokloster Castle, but the estate manager had not been informed of their visit. Thinking that they were two farm trainees, the manager lodged them with the other trainees and put them to work as common laborers. The next couple of days were spent working as simple farm hands with the only excitement occurring when Törni and Pitkänen let a garbage fire get away from them. Once the dowager arrived, the lodging situation quickly changed and the two Finns were held in awe by the Swedes who learned of their extensive combat experience.

After a short idyllic stay at Skokloster, Törni and Pitkänen went back to Stockholm where they spent the next two months. But, the two Finns were not prudent and got into some minor trouble. When their passports were checked by the Swedish police, the Finns learned that their visas were not stamped for an extended stay. Both Pitkänen and Törni were quickly deported back to Finland. Immediately upon their arrival in Finland, Törni was whisked back to prison, Pitkänen was detained for questioning. The Finnish government was embarrassed about the whole matter and Pitkänen was taken to police headquarters at Ratakatu. Three Finnish policemen grilled Pitkänen about everything imaginable. Fortunately for Pitkänen, he had met one of the policemen previously. One of the policemen was called away to answer a telephone call. The second policeman, a dedicated Communist, then went to the restroom, leaving Pitkänen with the third policeman. The third policeman, the acquaintance and a patriot told Pitkänen shortly after the others had left, "I'm going too. The door is open. See to it that you won't be here when I return!" Pitkänen made good his escape and was never brought back for further interrogation.

Despite receiving another two years added to his sentence for escaping, Törni began to plot his next escape. For him, there could only be freedom—no matter the cost. His next escape plan came to naught when a guard who was going to help him balked because of his concern for his family.

Far from being discouraged, Törni just kept planning and thinking. The incident with the guard was seen by Törni as a valuable lesson. He resolved that he would never again depend upon anyone else's assistance and that he would escape through his own efforts. Once this was resolved in his mind, he began to cast about for new escape routes.

Working in the prison's metal shop, Törni's fertile mind hit upon a novel escape idea. Due to his genial nature and good behavior, and the fact that he was not a criminal, he was popular with the prison population. This created a dilemma for the prison officials who were used to dealing with prisoners who were hardened criminals, not political ones. Törni's charming nature attracted the friendship of the prison chapel's organist. The prison chapel was on the third story of a building which offered an excellent view of the prison yard. While serving as an assistant to the organist, Törni observed and pieced together his next escape plan. There were many questions, but Törni bid his time and slowly answered each one.

If he escaped from the chapel window, he could cross the yard and scale the far wall. Once the wall was scaled, he would be able to avoid the guards and escape. If only there was a rope? Törni hit upon the idea of making a rope from his bedsheets and a grappling hook from scraps in the metal shop. The plan began to come together as Törni assembled the materials for his escape. On one occasion, the organist made note of Törni's odd collection of items, but Törni was able to explain their existence. Meanwhile, he worked on his escape plan and materials when it was possible and hid them behind the organ in the chapel.

The night of his escape finally arrived. Törni had planned for every detail except for the frequency of the guard's patrols. Like many of history's greatest generals learned, he determined that a good plan, instituted now, was better than an excellent plan later. Staying late one evening to take care of some feigned tasks for the organist, Törni quickly tied off his makeshift bedsheet rope and lowered himself out of the third story chapel window. Things initially went well for him, at least until the rope broke. Törni fell and landed hard on the dark prison yard below. While he did not break any bones, he severely sprained his ankle.

Undaunted, Törni hobbled painfully on and tried to scale the outer wall with his other makeshift rope and grappling hook. Time and again, the hook wouldn't grab, and the time quickly passed. Repressing the urge to panic, Törni knew that he must hurry. In the distance, he heard the returning guard's footsteps. Taking his rope and hiding, he allowed the guard to pass and then tried to scale the wall again. Finally, on one of his throws, Törni's grappling hook caught in the barbed wire's metal frame with a loud clang. Not wasting time, Törni desperately began to climb as the guard returned to the source of the noise. According to Törni's later account to his friend Colonel Kairinen:

We stood for a moment face-to-face without moving, but I was too far to suddenly surprise the guard and knock him to the ground. The guard chambered a round into his pistol, but it apparently went in crossways because the weapon did not fire. The man started to run to alert the other guard who was a couple of hundred meters away in the guard tower. As the guards began to converge from every direction, I raised my hands and surrendered.

Törni's third escape attempt had failed and he awaited a new addition to his sentence. But, the political climate in Finland had begun to change. The Finns were getting on with their lives and even the Communists had grown weary of their constant clamor against Fascism. People's lives began to dominate their thoughts, not the memories of the war. Because of this, Törni never received an addition to his sentence for attempting his third escape. In fact, he was treated better and was finally allowed to have visitors. From the depths of his despair, hope sprang anew.

In a complete surprise, Törni was awakened by a guard and led to the assistant warden's office several days before

Christmas Day, 1948. Reporting in his usual military manner to the assistant warden, he was notified that he had officially been pardoned by the new conservative President of Finland, J.K. Paasikivi. Quickly recovering from his initial shock, Törni was released from the Riihinaki State Prison a somewhat free man.

Törni made his way from Riihinaki to Helsinki where he was joyously reunited with his family. The celebration of his freedom lasted for several days, but Törni was impatient. He had come to realize that he would never be free in Finland. He had done nothing wrong, but he could never live in peace. The government could come and arrest him again and his past would always hang over his head.

The Communists continued to clamor for Törni to be tried for additional war crimes. It was only because the conservatives had been elected to the Finnish government that he was free. Even though he had been pardoned, Törni was still ordered to serve a supervised parole. He was forced to endure a 10:30 p.m. curfew and to meet weekly with a parole officer who reviewed his activities. He would have to seek his freedom, and on New Years Day, 1949, Lauri Törni realized that his future was in America. Other members of the Asekätkenta had escaped to America, so would he. It was his destiny...

With money provided by his father, Törni and his friend, Holger Pitkänen, travelled to Sweden again crossing the bridge at Haparanda in February 1949. Törni was also rumored to have continued on into Norway, but he eventually returned to Stockholm and Upsala, Sweden. While in Stockholm, Törni met the love of his life, a Swedish-American girl named Marja who fell deeply in love with him. It was a whirlwind romance as Törni proposed marriage to the young woman and she happily travelled to Helsinki where she got Törni's army uniform from his parents in preparation for their wedding. Photographs at the time showed a handsome Captain Törni dressed in his bemedaled uniform with a beautiful dark-haired girl. Both

Törni and his fiance, Marja. Stockholm, Sweden, early 1950. (Courtesy of Petri Sarjanen).

looked to be deeply in love with each other. But, happiness eluded Törni as the engagement failed and the two lovers parted company. The girl tried to correspond with Törni into the late 1950s, but he continued to pursue adventure rather than love. Her letters, although delivered by his Finnish friends, went unanswered until they eventually ceased.

Törni, now needing money, went into northern Sweden where he worked for a period as a lumberjack. He was well known to the Swedish police and intelligence services by identifying various Communists operating within Sweden. At one time, he was given a stipend by the Swedish Army to write several manuals about guerrilla warfare operations and the training he had received in Germany. Eventually, he obtained enough money to continue on with his plans to immigrate to America. The easiest way to get to American was by ship, but how? Once more, his old friend, Holger Pitkänen solved the problem by borrowing his cousin's seaman's papers. Holger's cousin, Eino Morsky, was a merchant marine sailor who had recently married and did not wish to return to the sea. Embracing Pitkänen for a last time with tears in his eyes, Lauri Törni now assumed the identity of **Eino Morsky**, a merchant seaman, and shipped out of the port of Gottenborg, Sweden on the S.S. Bolivia in May 1950 bound for Venezuela and more adventures.

8

ADRIFT

L auri Törni had assumed the identity of Eino Morsky, the Finnish merchant sailor. Now 30 years old and in good physical shape, Seaman Morsky did his job and nothing else to attract the attention or interest of the rest of the crew of the Swedish tanker S.S. Bolivia sailing towards Venezuela. Nobody knew his true identity or intentions, but Törni continually thought about how he would get to America. The time at sea passed quickly and the S.S. Bolivia soon berthed in La Guaira, Venezuela. Seaman Morsky went ashore at the port of La Guaira some time around late May 1950 and never returned.

Because of the massive number of foreigners who wanted to immigrate to the United States after World War II, the United States severely restricted the number of European immigrants allowed to enter. Strict quotas and tough immigration requirements were established for Europeans wanting to immigrate to the United States during this period. However, this was not the case for foreigners who wanted to immigrate from other parts of the world—particularly South America.

At first glance, it seemed ludicrous for a blond-haired, blue-eyed Finn who did not speak Spanish to go to Venezuela, let alone immigrate to the United States from there. But Eino Morsky had chosen his course carefully. While in Sweden, Morsky had inquired about immigrating to the United States. When he learned that his inquiry would be referred to the Finnish government, Morsky quickly gave up on that idea. Morsky had an old friend and former commander during the Winter War, Colonel Matti "Motti-Matti" Aarnio, who lived in Venezuela. Colonel Aarnio had carefully sponsored his friend's passage and immigration from Sweden to Venezuela. Next, many of the Asekätkenta who had fled the purges in Finland went to Venezuela from Sweden and then had obtained passage on to the United States. Finally, a large number of expatriate Finns lived in La Guaira and the nearby capital city of Caracas.

The Finns, being a clannish and private people, tend to congregate in small colonies when they live outside their native land. In these small cultural associations, the Finns assist each other, while keeping their language and culture alive. So it was in Venezuela. Morsky, with his easy and charming manner was quickly accepted into the local Finnish community. Törni continued to maintain the identity of Eino Morsky and was soon working as an electrician, handyman, and carpenter for many of the local Finns. Always the adventurer, Morsky could have easily gone to work in the nearby oil fields or prospected for gold and jewels in South America. Had he done so, he probably would have lived an obscure, and more than likely, wealthy life in this new land. But he continued to dream and scheme, almost as an obsession, on how he would get to America. Morsky had kept in touch with his Asekätkenta friends now serving in the US Army. For Morsky, only the United States offered the life and the freedom he sought. While life was certainly not hard in Venezuela, it was just another stopover of undetermined length on his journey to America. Besides, the Americans had just entered into the Korean War. If only he could get to America, Morsky reasoned, he could join the US Army and fight the Communists in Korea. Surely the Americans would be happy to have a man of his experience and abilities to fight the Communists.

After living approximately six months in Venezuela, he made the acquaintance of a fellow Finn who worked as a representative of an American steamship company which sailed between Venezuela and the United States. Morsky continually asked his friend for a job on one of the ships steaming to America from Venezuela. Finally relenting, the friend contacted still another Finnish friend who obtained Morsky a job as a seaman on the Norwegian freighter, the S.S. Libre Villa, which sailed between Venezuela and various American Gulf ports hauling ore for Alcoa Aluminum. But there were conditions attached to his employment. The main condition was that Morsky could not go ashore if the ship docked in the United States until he had worked for the steamship line for at least two months. This was a current restriction imposed upon the shipping company by the Americans. Without hesitation, Morsky promised that he would obey the rules and was soon signed aboard the S.S. Libre Villa as an able-bodied seaman.

9

A STRANGER IN A NEW LAND

The familiar tasks of being at sea kept Morsky physically busy, but mentally he was plotting his next move. Time passed quickly as the ship sailed the Caribbean Sea and arrived in Mobile, Alabama on 20 September 1950. As the ship entered the harbor, Morsky jumped overboard and swam ashore. Uncharacteristically, Törni had never intended to keep his word made in Venezuela prior to his voyage, but he had no regrets for the false promises.

Once ashore, Törni obtained dry clothes and took a Greyhound bus to Atlanta. At Atlanta, Törni purchased a commercial airline ticket and flew to Washington, D.C. From Washington, D.C., he took a train to New York City. Although he did not speak English, Törni was not slowed down as he put his plan into action. He was now in America, and he was free!

In New York, Törni miraculously met a fellow Finnish-American in Harlem who spoke his language. This Good Samaritan took Törni to the Imatra Society, a Finnish cultural and social gathering spot for Finns in New York City. As earlier in Venezuela, he was now amongst his own people. The Finns helped their new brother obtain employment and a place to live while assisting him in contacting his friends who were now serving in the US Army. Törni was able to contact friends such as Paavo Kairinen and Aito Keravuori; both of whom had been active members of the Asekätkenta and were now serving in the US Army. Lieutenant Colonel Alpo K. Marttinen and the other members of the "Marttinen Men" soon heard of Törni's arrival and planned for him to join them. Initially, he worked at Bakery Cafeteria in New York, Del-Rae Construction Company (Amityville, Long Island, NY) and took various temporary jobs working as an electrician and carpenter. He followed the example of another former sailor, Matti Jokinen, who had founded a construction company a few years earlier after working as a carpenter.

Colonel Alpo K. Marttinen, Knight of the Mannerheim Cross, 1944. (Courtesy of LTC Raimo Vertanen, Foundation of the Knights of the Mannerheim Cross).

America in the early 1950s was caught in the paranoia of the "Red Scare" with spies, saboteurs, and Communists seen "everywhere." On 19 June 1951, Törni got into a minor fight after a dispute with some blacks while working as a carpenter in Harlem. The New York Police Department responded to the fight, then the FBI somehow got involved, and arrested and jailed him. The Immigration and Naturalization Service (INS) was also contacted. He must have appeared to be a threat at the time. Here was a man who was obviously a foreigner, didn't speak English, could not prove his identity and had entered the United States illegally.

Fortunately, Törni had earlier made the acquaintance of a Mr. Paavo Fleming through the Imatra Society. Mr. Fleming was a former Finnish diplomat who had chosen to remain in the United States after World War II and was also the chairman of the Finnish War Veterans of America. He knew about Törni's legendary exploits in the Finnish Army and took a personal interest in this unusual young man.

News of Törni's arrest by the FBI came to Fleming who contacted a friend who was an attorney in New York. Being a former Finnish diplomat and currently employed as a caretaker for a wealthy family's estate, Fleming had many friends in New York. But this was not just any friend, and certainly not just any attorney. Paavo Fleming's friend was none other than the legendary General William "Wild Bill" Donovan who had retired from government service and returned to being a Wall Street attorney. General Donovan, a Congressional Medal of Honor winner with the "Fighting 69th" in World War I and the founder of the Office of Strategic Services (OSS), still carried a great deal of political clout. During World War II, Donovan's OSS was America's premier intelligence service, and he had overseen the formation of the Central Intelligence Agency (CIA) in 1947.

Fleming asked for an appointment with Donovan at his law offices of Donovan and Associates in New York City.

During the meeting, Donovan learned about the exploits of Lauri Törni and his present predicament. Fascinated, Donovan vowed to assist Törni and assigned one of his legal associates to represent his needs. Meanwhile, Törni languished in FBI custody.

The FBI and the INS relentlessly interrogated Törni. Instead of settling their fears, the twists and turns of Törni's life only raised more questions and concerns. Törni was vigorously interrogated about his service in the Finnish Army and actions against the Soviets. When it became known that he had been trained in Germany, both the FBI and the INS increased their pressure upon him. Somehow, the INS obtained copies of the lurid Finnish newspapers which had circulated during "The Great Treason Trial" in 1946 which claimed that Törni had been a member of a German unit called the "Sonderkommando Nord." This was a masterful stroke of Communist disinformation and the INS confused the Finnische Freiwillige Bataillon der Waffen SS Nordost with the Sonderkommando Nord. Unlike the Finnish officer training battalion, the Sonderkommando Nord was a special paramilitary unit which followed the spearhead German units during the invasion of Russia. Operating near Leningrad, the Sonderkommando Nord occupied captured Russian territory and exterminated "undesirable elements" such as Jews and Gypsies through mass executions and mobile gas chambers. Working in conjunction with the SS Einsatzgruppe, the Sonderkommandos used foreign volunteers, such as Latvians and Ukrainians, to wipe out whole populations.

Despite Törni's vehement denials, the INS suspected for a long time that Törni was a member of the Sonderkommando Nord. The FBI grilled Törni about his specialized training at Neustrelitz. Time and again, Törni was accused of being a spy who had been sent to the United States to conduct intelligence operations. Over and over, Törni was asked if he knew Morse Code, and if he knew how to conduct radio communications. He provided extensive written, sworn statements denying the accusations made by the INS and FBI. Törni wrote that he detested Fascism and Nazism, denied that he had ever been a Communist and swore to his love for the United States. Both the INS and the FBI looked for any inconsistency in Törni's story, no matter how inconsequential. Whenever an inconsistency was determined, Törni was immediately confronted and hammered with accusations of being a liar. For days at a time, Törni did nothing but attempt to remember events and answer questions.

Word of his predicament spread like wildfire through the former members of the Asekätkenta serving in the US Army. Major Kairinen and others wrote reams of notes and testimonials about both the character and exploits of the incarcerated Törni. This, along with a Habeus Corpus delivered by Donovan and Associates, quickly got Törni out of jail and away from the FBI. While incarcerated, Törni had to provide the FBI with an extensive 15-page written sworn statement regarding his entire life. Törni's sworn statement subsequently disappeared since recent Freedom of Information Act requests to the FBI by the author resulted in denials that any files were maintained by the FBI.

Important people became interested in the former Finnish jaeger. J. Edgar Hoover, Director of the FBI, was interested as were other influential people in Washington, D.C. as Törni's dossier was passed around. Kairinen and Marttinen knew of Törni's talents, and knew that they must act quickly if they were to secure his unique skills for use by the US Army or risk Törni being deported back to Finland.

Marttinen had the ear of such influential men as General William C. Wedemeyer and Senator Arthur Vandenburg. Donovan was not shy about contacting his associates on behalf of Törni.

With the help of the others, Törni obtained a work permit and returned to being a carpenter working for the Woodmere

Manor Company (Idlewilde, Long Island, NY) and Star Construction Corporation (NYC). Even though Törni outwardly displayed no concern towards his predicament, he was very concerned about his future. His immigration problems had not been resolved. Nothing was sure, and Törni knew it. Donovan and his law firm continued to represent Törni. On 22 February 1952, the INS served Törni with a notice of pending deportation. Törni was informed that he would shortly be deported from the United States and returned to Finland. In desperation, he applied to several countries, including Canada, for entry, but was denied on all accounts. By July 1952, several hearings regarding Törni's plight were held. Earlier in 1950, the Finnish Government had removed Törni's name from the roll of active Finnish Army officers and the Suopo (formerly the Valpo) made his extensive police records known to the Americans. True to his earlier predictions, the Finnish Government continued to make their presence felt in his life although he had left almost three years before. Finland wanted Törni deported from the United States and returned to Finland. Since 1949, the Finnish Communists had aggressively pressed for a new war crimes trial against Törni. He now felt that he had made the right decision to leave Finland and seek freedom in the United States. Törni had confided in Mr. Fleming the reason for his fear of deportation back to Finland. Mr. Fleming conveyed those fears of being tried as a war criminal to Mr. Donovan.

It seems that early in the Continuation War, Törni and his soldiers had attempted to capture some Soviet soldiers who had indicated that they wanted to surrender. Lulled by the display of a white flag, Törni and his soldiers had barely survived the Soviet ambush. From then on, Törni and his soldiers never took Soviet prisoners again for the rest of the war. He explained that his unit was too small and in too dangerous circumstances to be expected to drag along Soviet prisoners.

In truth, Törni sought out Soviet political commissars and members of the NKVD (precursor of the KGB) for brief and brutal interrogations. When Törni obtained the information he desired, he executed the prisoners. In one case, early in the Continuation War, Törni interrogated and then shot the prisoners. Several of Törni's men objected to what they considered cold-blooded murder, but Törni ignored them. These men resigned from Törni's command and returned to their parent regiments as soon as they returned to Finnish lines. The war was brutal on both sides, and Törni easily justified his conduct. He knew of the fate of numerous Finns who had been taken prisoner by the Soviets and questioned while having a cartridge case hammered through their kneecaps—then murdered by a shot through the head, bayoneted, or burned by the NKVD who were no longer amused with their sufferings.

Through these immigration hearings, his life was once again scrutinized as the Americans determined whether he was suitable to remain in the United States or should be deported. Throughout all of these interrogations, Törni told the truth about his life and willingly cooperated with the Americans. Törni attempted to curry favor by identifying Finnish Communists who were operating in the United States. Time and again, Törni let it be known that he only wanted to volunteer for service in the US Army to fight the Communists in Korea.

Various sources have claimed that Törni was a contract employee with the CIA during the early 1950s; however, no evidence has been found to substantiate such claims. While others argued his fate, Törni was placed on supervised parole which required him to report to the INS monthly but allowed to continue to work in New York City as a carpenter.

Finally, in 1953, Donovan was able to have a special private bill sponsored in the Congress of the United States of America. This bill, known as LEX TÖRNI (Private Bill HR

6412), was passed by the 83rd Congress on 12 August 1953 and read as follows:

> *Be it enacted by the Senate and House of Representatives of the United States of America in Congress assembled, that for the purposes of the Immigration and Nationality Act, Lauri Allan Törni shall be held and considered to have been lawfully admitted to the United States for permanent residence as of the date of the enactment of this Act, upon payment of the required visa fee. Upon the granting of such alien as provided for in this Act, the Secretary of State shall instruct the proper quota-control officer to deduct one number from the appropriate quota for the first year that such quota is available.*

Approved August 12, 1953

LEX TÖRNI allowed him to become a resident alien unencumbered by the American immigration laws, policies, and/or the restrictive quotas of the time. Törni was finally safe from deportation and on his way to becoming a US Citizen.

On 28 January 1954, he raised his right hand, took the solemn oath to "support and defend the Constitution of the United States," and formally enlisted in the US Army for a period of six years under the provisions of the Lodge Act. Törni had used the Norwalk, Connecticut address of his boss and friend, a Mr. Frederickson, as his military home of record.

10

BUCK PRIVATE

Like millions of other recruits before and after him, Recruit Lauri Allan Törni arrived at Fort Dix, New Jersey aboard a chartered bus in February, 1954 and was assigned to Service Battery, 34th Field Artillery for Basic Training. Despite his mental preparations, he was unprepared for the American training style and the sights which greeted him upon his arrival. Nothing could prepare him for the screaming, the pushing, the rushing from one place to another as he drew his equipment and bedding, along with getting the infamous "recruit" haircut and all of the painful medical injections. As anyone who has ever endured it will tell you, Basic Training was organized chaos which kept you confused, tired and hungry for the entire 12 weeks it took to transform a person from a civilian to a soldier.

The US Army of the 1950s was composed of mainly draftees, those young men who were selected by local Draft Boards to serve a compulsory two years active service in the armed forces. Some of the recruits were college educated, while others were allowed to serve in the Army rather than do time in jail. They were all mixed together in a Basic Training platoon. Added to this, there were the Lodge Act recruits like Thorne who were foreigners allowed to join the US Army with the promise of US Citizenship after 5 years of good service. While Törni tried to avoid anyone's attention, he seemed to draw it. First, he spoke fractured English even though he had been in the United States for nearly four years. Secondly, he was nearly 35 years old while the other recruits averaged about 19 years old, and he was in excellent shape.

The Korean War had just ended, and World War II ended less than 10 years before, so many of Törni's instructors were tough, no nonsense, combat veterans who enforced strict discipline. These were the days when the US Army was filled with "Professional Privates" and career Non-Commissioned Officers. It was also a time when the United States produced probably the finest army that it has ever had, only to see it destroyed by the excesses of Vietnam.

Törni, as was his habit, enthusiastically participated in the training. The old skills and habits of being a professional soldier quickly returned. He was not bothered by the cold weather, kitchen duty, calisthenics, long hikes with equipment, endless running, and the obstacle courses. All were challenges to be overcome, not merely tasks to be performed. While others endured, Törni thrived, especially when he was able to fire weapons and detonate explosives. He was once again doing his "desired work." But, the US Army also put its distinctive mold upon Törni before he departed Fort Dix. Törni's fractured English was now heavily spiced with obscenities and became a distinctive language that he learned while in the American barracks. From now on, Törni's sentences, uttered in a deep and booming voice, would be laced together with phrases such as "Shit" or "By God Damn."

By May 1954, Private Törni graduated from Basic Training and volunteered to attend the Mountain and Cold Weather Training Course at Fort Carson, Colorado. This highly demanding seven week course, taught the volunteers how to conduct military operations and survive in the unforgiving Rocky Mountains. Törni was again in a familiar world as he learned how the US Army skied, climbed mountains, operated in the winter, and survived in the cold. The altitude, cold, and deep snow challenged the volunteers. Once more, as others endured, he thrived. While Törni was not Airborne qualified at the time, he somehow got involved with the testing of parachutes at high altitudes. As a human guinea pig, Törni parachuted into the Rocky Mountains while testing new military parachutes and techniques. His parachute landings were frequently fast and hard in the thin mountain air. He was often dragged on the ground until he could get out of his harness. Yet, he relished the challenges and the danger.

Meanwhile, Törni stayed in contact with his Finnish former Asekätkenta friends who were also serving in the US Army. Several of these friends and their families were stationed at Fort Carson, so he was able to socialize with them when he had free time. Törni often visited Lieutenant Colonel Alpo K. Marttinen's family where he delighted Marttinen's wife and children with wild tales of his adventures, while Marttinen would silently glare his disapproval of such antics. As in Venezuela, the Finns enjoyed gathering to share their meals and native language. Photographs of Törni at the time show a lean, tanned and physically fit soldier looking resplendid in a starched khaki uniform surrounded by other happy Finns. Knowing Törni's talents and abilities, Lieutenant Colonel Marttinen, Major Kairinen, and other former Asekätkenta members pressed for the US Army to commission him as an officer. They had fears about his future. Unfortunately, their pleas fell upon deaf ears and Törni remained an enlisted man.

Completing the Mountain and Cold Weather Training Course and the parachute testing activities in September 1954, Private First Class Törni was ordered to Fort Benning, Georgia to formally attend Airborne training. When asked later why he had volunteered for Airborne and Special Forces training, Törni answered with characteristic understatement: "I decided that the Airborne and Special Forces might be more interesting (than regular units), and I thought I had the right kind of experience."

Arriving at Fort Benning, Georgia, assigned to the 1st Student Regiment (Jump School), Törni was issued his equipment and new jumpboots and found himself awaking early in the morning for quick, long-distance runs, and hours of calisthenics while learning the skills of American military parachuting. In the 1950s, the Airborne was the elite of the US Army, and was a tough club to join. According to a saying of the time, to be Airborne, one had better hack it or pack it. He learned to ask himself, "What if...?" and then develop endless contingency plans in case the unexpected somehow occurred. After the training, Törni completed his five bone-jarring T-7 parachute jumps and earned the right to wear his silver jumpwings proudly on his chest.

Törni no sooner graduated Airborne School than he reported to Smoke Bomb Hill, Fort Bragg, North Carolina. He received orders for a new secret unit called, "Special Forces." Törni didn't know it at the time, but Marttinen, Kairinen, and Keravuori had succeeded in getting the US Army to assign Törni to Special Forces where his special talents could be used to their advantage.

In 1954, Special Forces was still rarely spoken of within the US Army. Formed in secrecy on 20 June 1952, the 10th Special Forces Group (Airborne) originally consisted of only 10 officers and men. But recruitment was conducted by word of mouth and candidates were invited to join. By November 1953, the 10th Special Forces Group (Airborne) had sailed in secrecy from Wilmington, North Carolina to eventually arrive at their new home of Bad Tölz, Bavaria, Germany. A cadre of Special Forces-qualified officers and men remained behind at Fort Bragg to continue training and formed the nucleus of the 77th Special Forces Group (Airborne).

Assigned to the 77th Special Force Group (Airborne) and awaiting training, PFC Lauri Törni stopped by to visit his old friend, Major Paavo Kairinen who had recently been assigned to Special Forces. Kairinen joyously recounted the reunion with Törni in his book, *Marttisen Miehet:*

> *The time passed rapidly in hard work. Brother Lasse's (Törni) affair left my mind. My request to get into Special Forces had been approved and I was already temporarily assigned to a training battalion as commander at Fort Bragg, North Carolina when a "superb looking soldier," or Private First Class Larry A. Törni reported to me. That was a most joyful reunion.*
>
> *I asked him to relate the main points of what had happened since our last meeting. Lasse's soliloquy took all afternoon. I heard such astonishing things that I could hardly believe that they were true!*

Upon the insistence of Kairinen and others, PFC Törni attended the 3 month Special Forces Qualification Course, also known as the "Q" Course. Many of his fellow students were officers or senior NCOs and must have thought that it was odd that a 35-years old PFC was attending the "Q" Course with them, but Törni quickly showed the error of their thinking and became a valuable asset to them. The qualifications just to enter the course were awesome. Since their formation, Special Forces has searched for mature soldiers willing to take unusual risks and assume responsibilities above and beyond their rank. Volunteers with specialized knowledge of overseas areas and foreign languages or those who had fled from Communist countries were actively recruited to assist in forming a bank of experience which Special Forces could draw upon. Each candidate was a volunteer, was airborne qualified, had passed an impressive battery of physical and medical tests, had obtained a secret security clearance, had their service records thoroughly screened, and were extensively psychologically tested. As one Special Forces slogan stated, "People join us not because we're different, but because they are!"

Training began in earnest as the Special Forces candidates were taught the lessons of guerrilla warfare which the US Army had learned since 1939. The instructors encouraged the students, but attrition began to take its toll the first day. Students who could not meet the minimum standards were told to go elsewhere. Special Forces did not want soldiers who would fall apart in combat or who fell apart when they were isolated and alone with little support. The students were expected to be physically and psychologically tough when they arrived—there was no preparation period. Long conditioning marches with heavy rucksacks, along with long runs with rucksacks were a regular part of the training schedule. "Time under the ruck" was a form of dues paying which all Special Forces candidates still share today. Candidates learned about small-arms (firearms), improvised weapons, demolitions, improvised demolitions, hand-to-hand combat, combat first aid, communications, small unit tactics, and psychological warfare. However, not all of the "Q" Course was dedicated to fighting. As one SF veteran put it, "We were the armed Peace Corps."

A large portion of the course was used to instruct the candidates on how Special Forces was organized and operated in the Special Warfare environment, along with the peaceful applications of Special Forces. Törni learned that many Special Forces missions are designed to prevent a guerrilla war by helping the targeted people learn how to defend their villages, raise better crops and livestock, live in a healthier environment, and economically improve their lives. Törni learned that Special Forces was more than just guerrilla warfare and killing Communists. He finally understood the wisdom and purpose of the training and readily absorbed everything that was presented.

As a culmination of his training, Törni and the other candidates were parachuted into the Uwharrie National Forest, North Carolina as part of Operation Robin Sage. Operation Robin Sage is a bond shared by all graduates of the Special Warfare Qualification Course and is a field training exercise where all of the candidates conduct guerrilla activities against an opposing force, usually made up of 82nd Airborne Division soldiers.

Everything the Special Forces volunteers had learned in their classes was now put to practical use in the field while being evaluated. For the next 10 days, Törni and his fellow candidates used all of their experience to attack and elude their pursuers, while making contact with other "guerrillas" who were often the local residents. Upon their return to Fort Bragg, Törni and the other surviving graduates were officially welcomed into Special Forces, where additional training began. Törni had been bitten by the lure of Special Forces. With no ties other than to the US Army, he now lived and breathed the mission of Special Forces.

11

SPECIAL FORCES

Major Kairinen had pulled strings within the 77th SFG(A) to ensure that PFC Törni was assigned to the best unit in the Group. While guerrilla warfare was not new to Törni, Kairinen wanted him to learn how the Americans conducted their operations. Törni was reminded by his friends to keep a low profile, listen, and learn. If Törni was unhappy about remaining an enlisted man, he never showed it. But to Törni's Finnish friends, this situation was intolerable. Lieutenant Colonel Marttinen and Majors Kairinen and Keravuori feverishly worked to obtain permission to have Törni become a US Army officer by attending Officer Candidate School. As Kairinen related:

We had to work quickly to make Captain and Mannerheim - Cross Knight Törni into a model US Army soldier. I understood the haste of the matter.

I feared that Lasse (Törni) could get stuck on the step of non-commissioned officer unless he soon could demonstrate his skills, talent and experience. Lasse had to be made a US Army officer as quickly as possible.

Major Kairinen was in the process of being transferred to Europe, while Major Keravuori was attending the Special Warfare "Q" Course pending his assignment to Special Forces. It seemed as though nobody in the US Army had the vision to see the value of Törni as an officer. The Finnish government was not cooperating by not releasing Törni's military records, and had even removed Törni from their Officer's Rolls in 1950. Although this seems to be a trivial matter, in Finland such actions were a grave insult and were rarely performed. For the US Army, there was no real proof Törni had ever been an officer, only Törni's and the other Finn's verbal claims. He appeared to be trapped on the step of being an NCO as Kairinen had feared.

While this political maneuvering was occurring, Törni joined a Special Forces Operational Detachment - B or what is now known as a B-Team. The B-Team acts as a higher headquarters unit for approximately 10 Operational Detachment - As, or what is now known as A-Teams. A-Teams are the small operational teams which are the backbone of Special Forces. When Thorne joined his B-Team in late 1954/early 1955, B-Teams were known as FB Teams and were given an identity number such as FB-5 while A-Teams were known as FA Teams and were given an identity number such as FA-5 . The FB Teams were authorized to be manned by one officer and three NCOs to supply, administrate, and coordinate the activities of the A-Teams. The FA Teams were authorized to be manned by two officers and 13 NCOs, with a reduced strength of 13 men/officers if necessary. The 10th SFG(A) had gone to Germany earlier with FA Teams consisting of one officer and seven NCOs and reductions in the US Army's strength later brought the numbers down as low as one officer and six NCOs per each FA Team. Presently, an A-Team consists of the familiar one officer, one warrant officer and ten NCOs (2 & 10).

Serving in Special Forces in the early days was something close to being in the Foreign Legion. Many of the early members were Lodge Act soldiers with their thick, foreign accents, and often unpronounceable names. The 77th SFG(A) had Czechs, Finns, Poles, Hungarians, Irish, British, Dutch, Belgian, and even Germans assigned to their teams. There was a mystique, an aura surrounding service in Special Forces at the time. Many of the Lodge Act soldiers still had families behind the Iron Curtain, were very cautious about their past, refused to have their pictures taken, and often changed their names. Security was a way of life with these men, and their reluctance to talk about anything became almost a trait amongst the teams. Even to this day, many of the Special Forces "old-timers" will only say things such as, "One hell of a fine soldier!" That is all.

Törni found a home in the US Army. With a handful of strong, professionals in each team, there was informality and a strong sense of camaraderie between the officers and NCOs. Special Forces demanded total dedication and each man was required to perform at peak performance at all times. Teammates were treated with friendship, respect, and honesty. Stupid mistakes were quickly known by everyone. Soldiers who were identified as assholes tended to be regarded as assholes for the entire time that they were in Special Forces. While it was difficult to know everyone in Special Forces, it was not difficult to learn about someone in Special Forces. Team cohesion was important. While each soldier was highly trained in their own military specialty, they were cross-trained to a lesser degree in their teammate's military specialties; i.e., communications, medical, engineering, operations, light weapons, and others. Since the teams were expected to operate behind enemy lines without any real expectations of resupply, resourcefulness and improvisation were traits that were highly encouraged. Ultimately, the soldiers were expected to not only fight hard, but to teach their knowledge to others. The men in the teams learned and appreciated the value of their Lodge Act comrades since many of them had the skills and the languages that they were struggling to acquire.

In a short time, the 77th SFG(A) became very proficient with their new guerrilla warfare and instructor roles. However, it was always understrength. The phonies, the people who joined for the wrong reasons, and those who couldn't adjust were weeded out. Those, like Törni, who remained became stronger and more cohesive and attracted the same type of individuals. There was a shared fraternity where toughness and hardships were the dues to be paid for membership. Everyone knew that there were no replacements on an operational mission. Physical fitness was expected and demanded since there was no room for weaklings or stragglers. The teams were soon engaged in training in the snows of Alaska; the mountains of North Carolina and Colorado, the swamps of Florida, and in the waters of the Atlantic Ocean. Willing to learn anything from anyone, the 77th SFG(A) teams crosstrained with Air Force, Navy, Marine Corps, and other US Army units becoming familiar with everything from skis to submarines. Besides the exercises, individual team members were required to learn foreign languages and become familiar with foreign lands and customs. They studied war plans, memorized locations of potential guerrilla bases, and escape and evasion contacts and studied a myriad of information necessary for an operational deployment.

Törni quietly thrived in adversity and was well regarded by his fellow enlisted men and officers. Among the others, he was reserved, never spoke about his life and was described by a barracks mate as "an outstanding soldier who is cooperative, reliable, trustworthy, conscientious, and efficient." On 26 July 1955, Corporal Lauri A. Törni again took the oath "...to support and defend the Constitution of the United

States..." and became a United States Citizen at Raleigh, North Carolina during a mass swearing-in ceremony. He even got his picture in the local newspaper, being congratulated by LTC Jesse G. Ugalde, commander of the 77th SFG(A), for becoming an American. Immediately upon becoming a citizen, Törni formally changed his name one last time to become **Larry Allan Thorne** (pronounced Thor-nee).

But, Thorne's friends were still pressing the US Army to commission him as an officer. Lieutenant Colonel Marttinen was still pushing despite preparing for his reassignment to the 8th Infantry Division in Germany. Major Kairinen was gathering recommendations and documentation to submit to headquarters to request Thorne's commissioning. In the fall of 1956, LTC Marttinen wrote to Sergeant Thorne and notified him of a third attempt to have him commissioned. LTC Marttinen had gone to Signal Corps command and had met with a Major General in an attempt to persuade him to have Thorne commissioned. Marttinen, after conferring with the general, provided him with Thorne's records, recommendations, and a memorandum about Thorne's experiences in Finland. Thorne had recently been deeply involved in the "TEARS" program whereby long-ranged patrols were now able to use radio communications over long distances. This involvement turned out to be the key which unlocked the door allowing Thorne to become a US Army officer. Sergeant Thorne was ordered to attend a conference at the Pentagon. Soon afterwards, he received his orders to attend the Signal Corps Officer Candidate School at Fort Gordon, Georgia.

Reluctantly leaving the 77th SFG(A), Sergeant Thorne became Officer Candidate Thorne and once more attended an Officer Candidate School course designed to make him an officer and gentleman. The harassment, training, and studying were old hat for Thorne who had endured much worse years before at Niinisalo and Stralsund. Elected by his classmates as "most popular," Thorne sailed through the course with outstanding grades. Upon OCS graduation, Thorne was

S/SGT Larry A Thorne @ 1956. 77th SFG (A) (Courtesy of Lindholm - Ventola Family).

1LT Larry A. Thorne @ 1959. 10th SFG(A). (Courtesy of Lindholm-Ventola Family).

directly commissioned as a First Lieutenant in the Signal Corps. He then completed the Signal Corps Officer's Basic Course at Fort Gordon, Georgia.

In early 1957, upon completion of the Basic Course, 1LT Thorne was assigned to the 511th Signal Battalion, 11th Airborne Division, then stationed at Fort Campbell, Kentucky. By the summer of 1957, Thorne and the 11th Airborne Division were redeployed to Augsburg, Germany where they were under the US Army European Command and served as the reserve for NATO-Central Europe. To say that the 11th Airborne Division was a tough unit would be a understatement. At the time, it was staffed with tough, professional paratroopers who worked and played hard. They had the nickname, "The Flying Assholes" and lived up to their tough reputation. Even an artillery battalion chaplain destroyed a Gasthaus by pushing the piano through a window after assaulting several other patrons.

Thorne thoroughly hated his new duties and wanted to return to Special Forces. He was not suited to the duties of a regular garrison military force and was bored. Both of his old comrades, Majors Kairinen and Keravuori were stationed with the 10th Special Forces Group (Airborne) at Bad Tölz, only a few hours away. Whenever possible, the Finns gathered in Bad Tölz to have dinner, drinks, and socialize. Thorne often travelled to meet his friends in record time by speeding on the autobahns. He loved fast cars and often drove beyond a prudent speed.

First Lieutenant Thorne was somewhat of a ladies' man. He kept himself in excellent shape, dressed well and was careful in his personal grooming. Now back in Germany, he was on familiar ground which began to work against him. His friends warned him against drinking too much and driving too fast on the autobahns, but Thorne disregarded their sage advice. Each of us has our own personal demons, and Larry Thorne was no different. Despite his genial nature, Thorne could become unpleasant when he drank too much and his demons got loose. One of his friends described Thorne as "volcanic," generally easy to get along with, but extremely dangerous to be around when he got angry or drunk.

The warnings all came to naught in 1958 when Thorne was entertaining a German girlfriend at a local Gasthaus in Augsburg. Sometime in the evening, approximately eight German males entered the same club and began taunting Thorne and his girlfriend in the belief that they were erroneously having fun with an ordinary American G.I. Warned by his girlfriend that these men were dangerous members of a local crime syndicate, Thorne and his girlfriend tried to ignore them. Finally, when the Germans' taunts and harassment became unbearable, a thoroughly enraged Thorne launched into action. The Germans were stunned at how big, strong, and nimble the target of their taunts had suddenly become. Besides his extensive training in hand-to-hand combat he had received in Special Forces, Thorne was also an expert boxer and a violent brawler who was willing to get physical when need be. He fought with his hands, head, elbows, knees, and boots while rarely leaving himself open to attack, and was prepared for the Germans to attack from the rear. Despite the odds, the Germans didn't stand a chance against the Finn who was venting his pent-up anger. Thorne proceeded to demolish the club and put four of the German criminals in the local hospital with very serious injuries while physically throwing three others out into the street.

In the aftermath of the brawl, the 11th Airborne Division commander wanted to court-martial Thorne for his conduct unbecoming an officer while the Burgomeister of Augsburg wanted to give Thorne a commendation for punishing the German criminals so severely. As usual, Thorne was rather indifferent to his fate, but in reality, his career was in serious jeopardy.

Only the direct intervention of his old friend, Major Aito Keravuori, at the 10th SFG(A) saved his career. Major Keravuori, upon hearing of the incident, knew that Thorne's career was in danger and went to the 10th SFG(A)'s commander to make a direct appeal to have Thorne transferred to Bad Tölz. Had the 10th SFG(A) been commanded at the time by anyone other than Colonel Michael "Iron Mike" Paulick, Thorne probably would not have been spared. But Iron Mike was no everyday commander. A tough, bald, short, barrel-chested, and aggressive West Point graduate, Paulick eventually made Brigadier General, but this was probably due to his military prowess rather than through his diplomatic skills. Colonel Paulick lived for Special Forces and talked about it to anyone who would listen. After listening to Keravuori's desperate pleas, Colonel Paulick obtained Thorne's immediate transfer from the 11th Airborne Division to the 10th SFG(A).

Despite the cool reception from Paulick upon his arrival at Bad Tölz and the personal warning that he was now being watched closely, Thorne was estatic at being back with Special Forces again. He had again arrived home.

NOTE: At one time, there was a rumor that Thorne had killed a Soviet double-agent. While the rumor was popularly whispered, the author never found any evidence of credibility and attributes the story to another one of the Thorne Legend.

12

THE WILD BUNCH

Thorne's fellow officers and men welcomed him to the 10th SFG(A). Many of the senior NCOs had served in both the 77th and 10th SFG(A)s and were aware of Thorne's abilities.

Upon being assigned as the team leader of an A-Team, Thorne began preparing for the missions he anticipated. The period of 1958 - 1962 were the years which established his legendary status within the US Army. Throughout the world, the West and Communism were locked in a battle for the heart and minds of the nations struggling to govern themselves after the Colonial powers had departed. France had lost Indochina and was engaged in a vicious guerrilla war in Algeria. Great Britain was involved in the Middle and Far East. Africa was ready to explode. Colonel Paulick anticipated many of the brushfire wars which soon erupted and drove the 10th SFG(A) to prepare for the future. The 10th SFG(A) soon began to receive missions in Africa and the Middle East, despite the 10th SFG(A) being designated for a European conflict.

Paulick insisted that the 10th SFG(A) make contacts with and learn from other special warfare units. The French airborne shared their experiences in Indochina and Algeria, while the British SAS shared their experiences in Malaya. The 10th SFG(A) was soon training with the West Germans, Italians, Belgians, Dutch, Danish, Norwegians, Iranians, Saudi Arabians, and other nations. Each country offered new adventures and advice which was readily evaluated by the 10th SFG(A). The 10th SFG(A) established a special bond and mutual friendship with the local Bavarian Germans around Flint Kaserne at Bad Tölz. Many of the unit's German wives were from the local area. On one occasion, the 7th Army intervened and stopped the election of the popular German - American Captain Ludwig "Blue Max" Faistenhammer as the mayor of Bad Tölz.

Sometime in 1958, Thorne was allegedly ordered to join Special Forces Detachment A (known as Det. A). Operating in civilian clothes, Thorne and the other members of Det. A conducted unconventional warfare and intelligence operations in both sides of Berlin. Inquiries to the Central Intelligence Agency (CIA) disclosed no ties between Thorne and the Agency. However, the CIA is reluctant to disclose any sources or relationships.

Thorne was now at the top of his form. By this time, he was an expert skier, expert boxer, experienced mountaineer, and qualified as a High Altitude Low Opening (HALO) parachutist and able to speak English, Finnish, German, Estonian, Swedish, and Norwegian. Standing at 5'11" and weighing 180 lbs, Thorne was still in extraordinary physical condition. Other strong men would physically wince in pain at the strength of his handshake. He was given to slapping friends on the back or giving them a vigorous, rib-crushing bearhug when he was pleased. Ordered to report to Paulick's office one day, Thorne was told that he would be the first American to attend the prestigious Italian Alpini Mountaineering School at the invitation of the Italian Army. Paulick was sure that Thorne would not fail, and Thorne had no doubt of his abilities.

The Italian Alpini Mountaineering School is one of the toughest in the world. Being the first American to attend was a burden upon Thorne, but one he did not avoid. The Italian Alpini soldiers are among the elite of the Italian Army and responsible for defending Italy from any invasion through the Alps. As with many other elite units, regimental history and tradition play an important role. Many of the Italian Alpini's soldiers and families have served for generations in the same units. Although an experienced mountaineer and trained with the German Gebirgsjaegers (Mountain Troops), Thorne found the course challenging and physically exhausting. Not only did he have to climb the Alps, but he had to conduct military operations in some of the harshest climate in Europe. Despite the challenges of the Alps and the Italian instructors, Thorne did not fail and became the first American to graduate from the school and won the right to wear the prized Alpini mountain hat with its distinctive black raven feather tassel. Not given to idle praise, the tough Italian Alpini were impressed with Thorne's abilities and professional conduct. He returned to Bad Tölz, a hero. He accomplished his mission, in spite of the fact of being nearly 40 years old.

By 1959, Thorne felt bold or was confident enough to return home to his native Finland on vacation. Carrying an American passport and a US Army identification card in the name of Larry A. Thorne, it is doubtful that the Finnish Government did not know his true identity. Yet, his visits in 1959, 1960 and 1961 with his family in Helsinki were quite pleasant and joyous. During the 1961 visit, Thorne did not enter Finland quietly. He arrived in Finland with his custom Alfa-Romeo sports car bearing American Forces Europe license plates and a USA plaque which drew attention everywhere he went. If there was trouble or tension with the Finnish authorities, Thorne acted as though he was oblivious to it. However, Paavo

Thorne on leave in Helsinki, Finland with his Alfa-Romeo sports car, before the accident, 1961 (Courtesy of the Lindholm-Ventola Family).

Thorne on leave in Helsinki, Finland, 1961, with Father, Mother, and sister Kaija's daughter (Courtesy of Mrs. Kaija Mikkola).

125

Kairinen attended his father's funeral several years later, and was reminded by the local Communists that his presence was still not welcomed in Finland under any circumstances. Old hatreds remained. It would not be until 1982 that Colonel Kairinen felt that Finnish politics had changed enough for him to return to his native land in retirement.

Within a few days of his arrival in 1961, Thorne received unwanted attention—from the police! Thorne and a former Finnish girlfriend had a few drinks and went for a drive in his sports car. Speeding through the streets of Helsinki in the Alfa-Romeo which had been described as "as subtle as a fart in church," Thorne proceeded to go the wrong way on a downtown one-way street and had a minor fender-bender accident with another car. While it was a minor accident, the Finnish police took a dim view of the whole matter. As in most Scandinavian countries, driving under the influence of alcohol is considered a serious crime. Thorne's American passport was confiscated and he was ordered by the police not to leave the country.

According to legend, Thorne showed up back at the 10th SFG(A) headquarters at Bad Tölz several days after his leave had expired without his car. It was noted that Thorne was dirty, smelled badly, was unshaven, and his clothes were soiled and torn. Allegedly, Thorne had left the sports car hidden with a friend in Finland and made arrangements to have it shipped back to Germany later. Undaunted by the loss of his passport to the Finnish police, and definitely not willing to avail himself of Finnish justice again, Thorne allegedly waited until just prior to the end of his leave and stowed away on a freighter bound for Germany. After docking in Germany, Thorne hitchhiked back to Flint Kaserne, arriving several days after his leave had expired. In true Thorne fashion, he had lessons to teach about his "exfiltration" from Finland and the whole matter of his being absent without leave was forgotten.

13

MISSION IMPOSSIBLE

On 27 January 1962, a US Army DeHavilland Otter belonging to the Military Assistance Advisory Group, Iran (ARMISH/MAAG) crashed into the high, rugged Zagros Mountains of northwestern Iran. Lieutenant Colonel Johnson, Major Carder, Captain Knotts, and Sergeant Porters were killed in the crash. An Iranian Army unit trained in mountain warfare was dispatched to recover the bodies, but they failed. The Shah of Iran, having very cordial relations with the West Germans, requested that they provide an elite German Gebirgsjaeger (Mountain Infantry) unit to recovery the men. The Germans failed too. Several unsubstantiated rumors have arisen about this crash. First, it was believed that the aircraft was couriering Top Secret code material and the crash was too close to the Soviet Union to hope that the material had been destroyed in the crash. Secondly, it was rumored that the Shah of Iran met President Kennedy shortly after the crash and expressed dismay at how the Americans left their own dead on the side of a mountain.

For whatever reason, on 1 June 1962, Captains Larry A. Thorne and Herbert Y. Schandler were summoned to the 10th SFG(A) headquarters where they received a Letter of Instruction (LOI) instructing them to make preparations for the deployments of their A-Teams to Iran. As it was a sensitive mission they were ordered not to wear their green berets or any sort of distinctive insignia nor to make any mention of US Army Special Forces involvement. Schandler and Thorne were warned, "You and your men are the direct representatives of this unit and the United States government. You will govern your actions and conduct to reflect the highest standards of discipline, appearance, and professional ability."

The LOI directed that Schandler was the commander of the reinforced detachment and the base camp, while Thorne was the commander of the high camp and responsible for the search and recovery efforts. They were tasked with the primary mission of recovering the bodies and equipment, and had secondary missions of destroying the wreckage along with conducting area familiarization and orientation; i.e., gathering intelligence. Schandler and Thorne were given 14 days to conduct the entire operation and warned not to expose themselves or their soldiers to undue risks to recover the bodies or equipment.

Schandler gathered his Detachment A-23 while Thorne gathered his Detachment A-2. Together, they briefed the soldiers on their mission and what to expect. Departing Neubiberg, Germany at 2030 hours aboard a USAF C-130 cargo aircraft on Friday, 1 June 1962, the recovery team arrived in Evreaux, France. At Evreaux, nobody had been informed of their arrival so no prior arrangements were made for food or lodging. However, a friendly US Air Force sergeant assisted the recovery team as best he could, and they went to sleep on the floor of a hanger after checking their equipment. The next morning, the USAF sergeant again obtained breakfast and transportation for the team.

Flying out of Evreaux on Saturday, 2 June 1962, the aircraft stopped at Chateauroux and then continued on to Athens, Greece arriving there at 1900 hours. As at Evreaux, there was no billeting or transportation arranged, but the USAF made arrangements for the recovery team to stay at local hotels and get a ride to the airfield on the next day.

Departing Athens on 3 June 1962, the recovery team finally arrived in Teheran, Iran at 1610 hours. After getting their equipment and baggage through customs, Schandler and Thorne arranged for the meals and billeting of their soldiers and then met with a liaison officer from ARMISH/MAAG. Over dinner, with members of the Iranian Army and ARMISH/MAAG, Schandler and Thorne discussed their plans. Lieutenant Colonel Barquist, US Army Hospital - Teheran, wanted the recovery team to depart Teheran the next morning, but Schandler and Thorne disagreed suggesting that it would be better if the next day was used to segregate and pack their supplies and equipment. Barquist was anxious to get started, but agreed to the stated plan.

Captain Larry A. Thorne on glacier in the Zagros mountains, Iran, 1962 (Courtesy Col. Robert Rheault via John Larsen).

Iranian horses and camels used to supply the Special Forces teams. The Zagros Mountains are in the background. (Photo courtesy of "L.G.").

A Special Forces staff sergeant in the Zagros Mountains with a M-2 carbine. (Photo courtesy of "L.G.").

The Otter's crash site in the Zagros Mountains, along with an unidentified Special Forces soldier. (Photo courtesy of "L.G.").

Detachment A-2. The "High Camp" Team in Tehran at the completion of the Zagros Mountain mission. Top (L-R): SFC Henry T. Belton, MSGT Charles F. Rhodes, Thorne, and SGT Ario Caravalho. Bottom (L-R): SSGT Jan Novy and SSGT Willis A Blair. (Photo courtesy of "L.G.").

The recovery team used the time to check and repack their supplies and equipment while Captain Schandler briefed various MAAG personnel and conducted protocol. Schandler left a Special Forces Lieutenant and NCO at Teheran to coordinate any air drops if further supplies were requested. Departing Tehran by military trucks, the recovery team made their way to the city of Esfahan. After performing some liaison tasks with the local Iranian Gendarmerie, the recovery team drove to the remote village of Kurang where they met with the local village chief. The chief showed the two captains where the base camp should be established and they haggled over the price for the mules that they needed to transport supplies.

The next morning, the recovery team packed 25 cases of C rations, water, demolitions, radios, and oxygen on the mules which had arrived. Colonel Barquist was quite insistent that water was available at the camp, and so, reluctantly, Schandler made the decision not to pack the water in.

After establishing the base camp, the high camp party (8 members) and the carrying party (11 members) were led by the tribal chief up the mountains towards the advanced camp. The advanced camp was established after a long hard day of climbing.

Since the mules could not climb any further, the Iranians were paid off and sent home. Thorne and a carrying party continued on lugging all of their own equipment themselves. The carrying party returned to the advanced camp and left Thorne and his team at the high camp. It was an exhausting day for everyone at altitudes of 14,000 feet. The crash had occurred approximately 20 miles from Kurang on the Zardeh Kur ridge. The most prominent point of the ridge was Shaigan Mountain (14,921 feet) and is Iran's third highest mountain. After final coordination with Thorne, Schandler and the others returned to the base camp near the village of Kurang.

On Saturday, 9 June 1962, Schandler received a radio message from Thorne saying that the high camp had located two bodies and needed water delivered. Fuel for the arctic stoves and water were air-dropped to Thorne the next day, but were improperly packed and most of the supplies were lost. During the period of 9-15 June, Thorne and his team recovered two bodies (Major Carder and Captain Knotts) and found equipment belonging to Sergeant Porters. Iranian tribal members, along with earlier rescue teams had scavenged the crash site making the search much harder. Thorne and his team recovered as much personal and aircraft equipment as possible and then destroyed the wreck with explosives and thermite. Schandler and members of his team brought the bodies down and transported them in coffins packed with ice to Esfahan. Contacting 10th SFG(A) headquarters at Bad Tölz by radio, Schandler received permission to remain until the other bodies were located and recovered.

Master Sergeant Charles Rhodes, the senior NCO of Thorne's team, located a third body (LTC Johnson) on 16 June 1962. Sergeant Porters' body was never located. Thorne notified the base camp and Schandler sent a team with mules to bring out the body. Schandler and Thorne agreed that further searching was futile, and Thorne's team was ordered to return to the base camp.

The mule team arrived the next afternoon and the body was prepared for transport by placing it in a rubber bag full of ice. Thorne and his men struck camp and the entire group left for the base camp near Kurang at 1630 hours, 17 June 1962. The troops marched all night, with only short breaks, and arrived at the base camp at 0300 hours, 18 June 1962.

Lieutenant Colonel Johnson's body was then repacked in a coffin full of ice and sent to Esfahan. By 0630 hours that morning, the base camp was struck and the recovery team boarded trucks to return to Esfahan. Before leaving Kurang,

Captains Schandler and Thorne paid their respects to the local Khan and exchanged presents.

The recovery team arrived at Esfahan that evening and stayed at the Hotel Esfahan. Departing early the next morning, the recovery team finally arrived at the ARMISH/MAAG motorpool at 1600 hours, 19 June 1962. After all of the equipment was cleaned and turned in, the troops stayed the night in a Teheran hotel.

On 20 June 1962, Schandler and Thorne, along with Barquist, called upon General Hayden and Colonel Tarkenton at ARMISH/MAAG where they presented an extensive debriefing of the entire mission. Meanwhile, the recovery team received a partial pay and turned in receipts for the expenses of the operation. Departing Teheran by military transport aircraft at 1500 hours, the recovery team arrived back at 10th Special Forces Group (Airborne) headquarters several days later. In his afteraction report, Schandler made the following comment:

The troops were somewhat disappointed that no representative from ARMISH/MAAG ever expressed a word of thanks to them or that no one from ARMISH/ MAAG was present to see them off.

The recovery mission had been tough, but was most valuable. Both Thorne's and Schandler's afteraction reports gave insights and valuable information about the region, the peoples of the area and conducting military operations in the Middle East. Thorne's mission at the high camp was an arduous struggle against nature and the elements. Besides the cold, windy, and barren environment, Thorne described the scene as:

The area was in the midst of a locust plague and the entire area was covered with them. Due to this the snow and water resulting from melting snow was considered to be contaminated. In places the snow was so covered with the dead locust that it was like walking in mud.

The majority of the Imperial Iranian Air Force's air-dropped supplies were lost due to poor packing techniques or landed a great distance from Thorne's location. Meanwhile, Schandler had met with the local village chief and the local Khan. With the permission of the local Khan, Schandler had his team medics conduct daily medical clinics for the local Bahtiari tribesmen. The results were phenomenal. Word about the American medics spread like wildfire and patients often walked two days to be examined. The Special Forces medics daily saw patients with conditions from headaches to tuberculosis and rotten teeth starting early in the morning and often going late into the night. The poverty-ridden Bahtiari were grateful for the care provided by the Americans and tried to repay them with food that they could ill afford to give away. The tribesmen were very grateful for the Special Forces' medics.

14

THE CALM BEFORE
THE STORM

Schandler, Thorne, and the members of the recovery team returned to Bad Tölz and reentered their routine of training and preparation. But the world was changing, and it was changing dramatically for Special Forces. With the rise of Wars of National Liberation, as prophesised by Premier Kruschev, and the interest of President Kennedy, the US Army and Special Forces began to review their tasks and missions. Special Forces had originally been formed to conduct guerrilla operations against the anticipated Soviet invasion of Western Europe. Now, the flames of revolution, often Communist-inspired or financed, spread around the world. Many revolutions were popping up around the world, and Special Forces was given the mission of preparing to conduct counterinsurgency warfare. Instead of becoming the guerrillas, Special Forces was now tasked to teach indigenous people how to fight the guerrillas. This was a major change in both mission and direction, but Thorne and the others in Special

Forces rose to the challenge. As soldiers returned to the 10th SFG(A) from "advisory" duty in a country in Asia called Vietnam, Thorne began to read and learn more. With the Cuban Missile Crisis of 1962, Thorne had a premonition that he would soon be fighting his sworn enemies again.

On 22 October 1962, Thorne was ordered to report to the US Army Infantry Center and School, Fort Benning, Georgia to attend the Associated Infantry Officer Course, Class 2 (now known as the Advanced Infantry Officer's Course). He realized that this course was necessary for his professional development, but was reluctant to leave the 10th SFG(A). Such courses were a way for the US Army to keep their officers current in tactics, doctrine, and policy while periodically bringing them back into the mainstream. Thorne didn't want to be part of the mainstream conventional Army, he'd had enough of that as a junior officer with the 11th Airborne Division. Staff officer—Hell no! Motor pool duties? No thanks. Thorne was quite content with staying in Special Forces, even if he were to remain a Captain and consoled himself with the thought that he would return to Special Forces upon completion of the Advanced Course.

If Thorne had expected a drab, academic environment upon his return to the Infantry School at Fort Benning, Georgia, he was wrong. As with almost any course, the instructors and fellow students often shaped the character of the instruction. Thorne picked a great class. AIOC #2 was a wild collection of regular and reserve US Army captains who studied hard and played even harder. Among Thorne's classmates was David Hackworth, Chuck Darnell, and Mike Phelan. The course was designed to teach the officers how to function within battalion staffs, along with a blend of leadership, and assorted field problems. There were also plenty of in-depth discussions about a variety of topics, and the students were encouraged to be frank. Thorne readily engaged in these discussions, particularly about the growing conflict in Vietnam.

He was quite outspoken about how the Americans would lose in Vietnam if they did not change their outdated and outmoded guerrilla tactics and become less reliant upon the helicopter. Even Captain Hackworth, one of the most decorated soldiers in the Korean War, sat up, listened to, and agreed with the now 43 year-old Thorne.

Despite the world tensions, and the course's academic demands, the class had time to play. One of the students, Captain Merle Bishop, was a Special Forces Reservist and owned a florist shop in Alexander City, Alabama. He owned a vacation home at nearby Martin Lake and invited his all-male classmates to have a blow-out weekend at the lake as his guest. It turned out to be quite a blow-out according to one of the participants, now-retired Lieutenant Colonel Mike Phelan:

> *Since it was near freezing, nobody took along their bathing trunks but after the consumption of significant quantities of alcohol, challenges began. Soon nude Special Forces-types were observed water-skiing on the lake in the dead of winter. Quite a few people live year-round or spend their weekends at their vacation homes—and the phone started ringing but surprisingly enough, all of the calls were favorable.*

Returning to Fort Benning without further incident, Thorne and his classmates graduated on 23 March 1963. Upon graduation, Thorne reported to the US Army Psychological Warfare Center, Fort Bragg, North Carolina and was assigned to the Training Group. As an instructor, he was now tasked with teaching Special Forces students going through the Qualification Course about guerrilla warfare.

15

A PERIOD OF INTRIGUE

As part of Training Group, Thorne was assigned to train Special Forces candidates in guerrilla warfare. His main duty was to act as an instructor and the guerrilla chieftain, "Charlie Brown," during Operation Robin Sage exercises. Now, nearly ten years after he had graduated from the same course, Thorne passed along his experience to the Q Course students. As the guerrilla chieftain, Thorne had the ultimate power to pass or fail any of the potential Special Forces students he evaluated. The lessons and tricks which he taught during this period are still being talked about with admiration by Special Forces veterans. Already well known in Special Forces circles, Thorne's unorthodox antics as the guerrilla chieftain "Charlie Brown" elevated him to a legend.

Thorne stressed that the success of any guerrilla group was mainly dependent upon the group's leader. He was particularly demanding of the young junior officers who were vying to become Special Forces qualified. Ill-led or ill-trained guerrilla bands cease to exist. Either they are destroyed by the enemy forces or the guerrillas become disillusioned and dissolve. He was looking for students who had the courage and ability to endure hardships and face death at any time while fighting against impossible odds. Thorne wanted leaders who were capable of creating an organized, functioning guerrilla force which was lean, mean, and hard-hitting rather than a disorganized, compromising force more comfortable in garrison than in the field. Common, basic operational functions of a guerrilla band were continually practiced in the field in order to be fully understood. Thorne didn't concern himself with strategic aims.

Thorne passed on that guerrilla leaders needed to be familiar with subjects ranging from human psychology to Morse code communications. The young Special Forces soldiers were forced to break the mind-set that they were still part of the regular Army which had unlimited supplies, staff advice, and other support. Thorne drilled into the students that guerrillas are isolated and must live by their wits, relying upon nobody else to help or save them. One wrong decision or action could easily destroy the entire guerrilla group. Under Thorne's demanding tutelage, it became apparent to the Special Forces trainees that once deployed in an operational detachment, they must depend upon two things: 1) Their Teammates and 2) Themselves.

On 31 October 1962, a female military dependent, employed by the Fort Benning Post Exchange Service walked into Columbus Field Office of the 111th INTC Group, Fort Benning. The woman, identified as "Source V-2", told the Army Special Agents that she was fairly certain that she had seen an individual at Fort Benning who resembled a Russian officer who had frequented a restaurant where she had worked in Paris in either 1948 or 1949. According to US Army documents recently released:

Source, who is known to the Columbus Field Office, is considered to be a level headed individual with no apparent ulterior motive in reporting the above information. She does not desire to be identified at this time until further investigation is made to determine whether or not she is correct in her assumption.

Greatly concerned that a possible Soviet agent was operating in their midst, the Special Agents notified their higher headquarters and began an intensive investigation to determine the identity of the individual reported by the female source. The Special Agents determined the name of their suspect: Captain Larry A. Thorne.

The released official reports painted a sinister portrait of Thorne. According to one Agent Report, dated 1 March 1963: On 21 February 1963, V-2 was interviewed and furnished the following information to this office:

In October 1962, Source, in her capacity as cashier of a cafeteria at Fort Benning, Georgia, observed a customer as HE was paying for HIS food who seemed familiar to her. Her attention was attracted to the man because of HIS Slavic features and the fact that HE wore a ring on HIS middle finger as the Russians frequently do. Source's attention was focused on SUBJECT as HE chose a table, seated HIMSELF, and began to eat. In Source's opinion, HE "ate like a pig," and HE drank milk from a cardboard carton without the use of a straw. SUBJECT reminded Source of a Russian officer whom she had seen once or twice in 1944 or 1945.

In 1945, Source, who is now 36 years of age, was employed as a waitress in a private restaurant which was located on the first floor of a five story building in Paris, France, on Rue de la Faisanderi near the Arch of Triumph. Near her place of employment in Paris, there was a large building which always had a Russian flag flying from the grounds, and Source believes that it was some type of Russian Military Mission. It was not unusual for some of the Russian officers to enter the restaurant where she was employed. The Russian officer who reminded her of SUBJECT had used the restaurant on one or two occasions in the winter of 1944-1945. Source never heard the Russian speak. She estimated that he was in his late 20s in 1945. In the summer of 1945, Source met her present husband, married him, and moved away from Paris. While SUBJECT was seated in the cafeteria at Fort Benning, Source who wanted to hear HIM in order to determine HIS accent, approached HIS table and asked HIM if HE had been in Paris at the end of World War II. SUBJECT gave her a negative answer by shaking HIS head. Source stated to HIM that HE reminded her of someone she had seen in Paris, and, at that time, SUBJECT informed her that she was mistaken. She then asked HIS pardon, excused herself, and left his table. Source estimates SUBJECT'S age at the present time as 38 or 40. Source has seen HIM in the cafeteria only once since that time. HE was alone on both occasions. Nothing has occurred since Source first saw SUBJECT at Fort Benning which would strengthen her belief concerning HIM, and there is no possible means by which she can identify SUBJECT.

Unknown to Thorne, since October 1962, he had been under investigation by the US Army for allegedly being a Communist spy. The Special Agents of the 111th INTC Group had received permission to conduct a full fledged investigation of Captain Thorne, and they vigorously investigated the waitress' allegations.

By March 1963, Thorne had finished the Advanced Course at Fort Benning and had transferred from Training Group to the 7th Special Forces Group (Airborne) and was now commanding Detachment A-18. On 12 July 1963, Special Agents attempted to locate and interview Thorne but he had departed for a 60-day temporary duty assignment (TDY) to Columbia, South Carolina in conjunction with Operation Swift Strike III and was not expected to arrive back to Fort Bragg, North Carolina until approximately 21 August 1963.

Returning from the 60-day Operation Swift Strike exercise, Thorne was ordered to headquarters. Arriving at the headquarters, the thoroughly bewildered Thorne was met by Special Agents of the Fayetteville Field Office, Region II, 111th Intelligence Corps Group acting upon orders from the Assistant Chief of Staff for Intelligence, Third Army, Fort McPherson, Georgia. By this time, Thorne's records from the Immigration and Naturalization Service (INS) had been requested, and records checked in Britain; the Columbus, GA Police Department; Columbus, GA Municipal Court; Columbus, GA City Court; Columbus, GA Superior Court; Phenix City, AL Police Department; Phenix City, AL County Court; Phenix City, AL Circuit Court; Fort Benning, GA 86th MP (CI) Detachment and the Fort Benning, GA Provost Marshal's Office. No rock was left unturned and no question was being left unanswered.

The Special Agents took Thorne to their Field Office where they immediately read him his rights under the Uniform Code of Military Justice (UCMJ) and informed him that he was under investigation per Article 31, UCMJ. Thorne was now in serious trouble. He willingly cooperated with the agents, and agreed to a polygraph examination in writing, but let it be known that he did not like his loyalty being questioned.

For days, the agents interrogated Thorne regarding the allegation that he was a Soviet spy or possibly even a Russian officer. On 29 August 1963, Thorne was given a polygraph test after he was allowed to review the extensive written statements which he had given the Special Agents days before. The polygraph results were recently released and show the intense sort of scrutiny and pressure that Thorne was under:

"Thorne was asked the following questions during the test and HIS answers were as indicated:

TEST I

1. Is today 29 August 1963? Yes.
2. Did you have a beer last night? Yes.
3. Other than United States Army maneuvers, have you correctly identified the names you have used? Yes.
4. Did you participate in Swift Strike III? Yes.
5. Other than what you told me, do you have any personal or official ties with former associates in the Finnish Army? Yes.
6. Other than the war years, were you ever in a Communist country? No.
7. Do you have any relatives in a communist country? No.
8. Are you a paratrooper? Yes.

TEST II

1. Are we at Fort Bragg, North Carolina? Yes.
2. Were you born on 28 May 1919 in Viborg, Finland? Yes.
3. Were you ever employed by Communist Security Police? No.
4. Were you ever in Paris, France prior to 1961? No.
5. Are you a professional soldier? Yes.
6. Did you ever wear a Russian uniform? No.
7. Were you sent to the United States to perform an intelligence mission for a foreign country? No.
8. Did you drink a cup of coffee this morning? Yes.

144

Prior to each test, each question was explained and discussed with the SUBJECT who stated that HE understood the questions. Before taking the test, THORNE stated that HE was willing to take the test but considered being required to take the test an insult. HE did not, however, at any time behave in any manner that was not most cooperative and HE followed all instructions implicitly. HE enjoyed good health and had taken no medication or suffered any illness in the several days preceding the test. No unexplained tracings appeared on THORNE'S charts and it is the examiner's opinion that HE answered all questions with what he believed to be the truth. No post test interrogation of SUBJECT was conducted because of the lack of deceptive tracings in HIS test charts."

Once more, investigators went over his entire life with a fine tooth comb asking questions about his aliases, his involvement with the Germans, his imprisonments and his life since coming to America. The interrogators again asked Thorne about this alleged involvement with "Sonderkommando Nord" and whether he had received any radio communications training from the Germans. All of his immigration records were again reviewed and he was closely questioned about their contents. His denials fell upon deaf ears. Time and again, he was asked to provide sworn statements about every facet of his life. Any and all contradictions, no matter how small and even obscure mistakes in memory were ruthlessly investigated. All of his polygraph tests showed no evidence of deception, and the investigator's reports stated that they believed him to be truthful. But like any allegation made in secrecy, this matter lingered on.

On 9 March 1965, the Office of the Assistance Chief of Staff for Intelligence wrote a memorandum for record regarding Thorne's investigation. It read in part:

A review of all available information discloses insufficient derogatory information within the purview of paragraph 14b, AR 604-10 (Military Personnel Security Program) to warrant processing this case under the provisions of those regulations. Case closed under the provisions of paragraph 27c, AR 604-10.

FOR THE ASSISTANT CHIEF OF STAFF

FOR INTELLIGENCE.

Despite the ACOSI memorandum for record, it took until 14 October 1965 before Thorne's investigation was closed by the Assistant Chief of Staff, G2, XVIII Airborne Corps, Fort Bragg, NC. The closure document stated:

1. Forwarded herewith for your review are results of recent investigation completed at Headquarters, Third U.S. Army, together with Central Records Facility dossier F8123963, pertaining to SUBJECT.
2. Investigation failed to confirm the allegation concerning SUBJECT set forth in inclosed Summary of Information, AJAGI-I 20, dated 14 December 1962. Accordingly, instant case has been closed favorably and no further action is contemplated.
3. Request this correspondence, together with attached investigative file and Central Records Facility dossier be returned to this headquarters on or before above suspense date.

FOR THE ASSISTANT CHIEF OF STAFF, G2.

Although relieved at being somewhat vindicated, Thorne was livid at having his patriotism and loyalty questioned. Accused of being a Communist was the ultimate insult to Thorne. Still, he returned to the 7th SFG(A) and began to prepare his

A-Team for an anticipated deployment to South Vietnam. Years before, he had come to America to fight the Communists in Korea, now he would be able to fight them in South Vietnam.

16

TEMPORARY DUTY

Thorne, during pre-deployment training, had driven his team hard. Even the recent assassination of President Kennedy only momentarily distracted him from his mission. He knew the dangers ahead, and relentlessly prepared himself and his team for combat. Together, they learned about the land, language, and customs of South Vietnam, along with honing their individual and team combat skills. Thorne was fanatical about contingency plans and standard operating procedures (SOPs). They practiced their plans and contingencies over and over. Everything from road marches to counter-ambushes was practiced in almost mind numbing detail. Thorne expected the best from his subordinates and accepted nothing less. Their lives depended upon it. After being isolated in preparation for deployment, Thorne's team, now redesignated Detachment A-743 was sent to the Republic of Vietnam for a six month temporary duty assignment (TDY) in November 1963. At this time, all Special Forces deployments to South Vietnam were six months in duration.

Thorne's A-Team was tasked to support the Civilian Irregular Defense Group Program. While the basic concept of the CIDG (pronounced "Cidgee") Program was conceived by the CIA, it was a Special Forces operation from beginning to end, and was created for two principle reasons.

1) The US Army determined that a paramilitary force be developed from South Vietnamese minority groups in order to strengthen and broaden the counterinsurgency efforts of the Republic of Vietnam Government.

2) The Montagnards and other minority groups were prime targets for Communist propaganda, particularly due to their dissatisfaction with their treatment by the Republic of Vietnam Government. If the Communists could recruit these groups, then they would have control over large and strategic areas.

The CIDG Program eventually involved thousands of Special Forces soldiers, hundreds of thousands of Vietnamese and minority group civilians, millions of dollars and over 100 camps spread from the Demilitarized Zone (DMZ) to the Gulf of Siam. In nine years of involvement, Special Forces became involved in every aspect of counterinsurgency warfare: economic, military, psychological, and political. The CIDG program involved teaching the Vietnamese and the minority groups how to shoot, farm, build, care for the sick, and deal with the various religious and ethnic differences. It was a story of countless small skirmishes and numerous large battles as small, isolated camps were carved out of the jungle or braced against the Mekong Delta floods. Both loved and reviled by both the Americans and South Vietnamese, the program was almost destroyed by its American creators. In the end, the CIDG program was a story of conflict, cover, and cooperation between a myriad of sometimes competing entities.

Early CIDG camps were really lightly defended villages. Their first operations were small local security patrols, ambushes, village defense patrols, local intelligence networks, and an alert system of local men, women, and children who reported any suspicious activities.

Specialized CIDG activities were begun where paramilitary units were formed as "mountain commandos" or "mountain scouts." These men and their Special Forces advisors conducted long range reconnaissance patrols in remote jungle and mountain areas. Another activity was the training and employment of "trail watchers." These border surveillance paramilitary units were formed to monitor and report Viet Cong (VC) movement near the border and to capture or destroy small VC units whenever possible.

The general mission of the CIDG camp was to train indigenous "strike forces" and village defenders; bring the local populace under the influence of the South Vietnamese government; employ paramilitary forces in combat operations to reinforce organized hamlets; carry out interdiction activities; conduct joint operations with the South Vietnamese Army to further CIDG operations; conduct psychological operations; establish an area intelligence system (reconnaissance patrols, observation posts and agent/informant networks); conduct a civic action program, and where possible, establish a border screening force.

Each border surveillance camp was authorized four striker companies. Two companies were supposed to be on the border at all times while operating from forward bases. However, this arrangement did not always work in real life. While the border surveillance camps had no real success in controlling VC movement across the border, the camps were still valuable for their surveillance missions, intelligence gathering abilities and continued to contribute to area development.

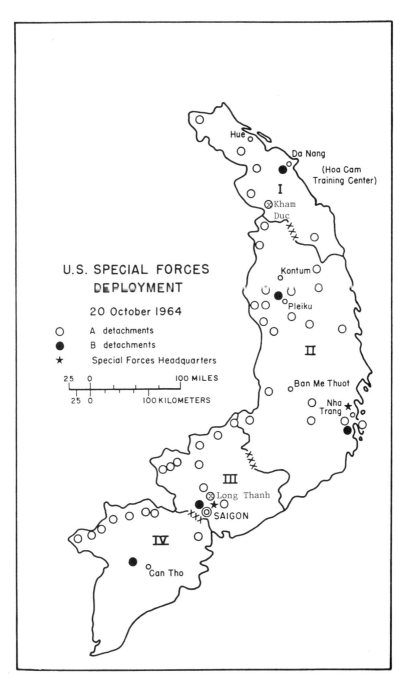

Map of Vietnam

Early Special Forces operations in Vietnam 1962. COL Richard Stilwell, Plei Do Lim, 1962. (Private Collection of the author via Larry Dring).

Map Check, Plei Do Lim, 1962.

S/SGT Larry Dring, Plei Do Lim, 1962.

Detachment A-743 arrived at Tan Son Nhut Air Force Base near Saigon, and was transported to the Special Forces headquarters at the coastal city of Nha Trang. After a short period of team acclimatization, familiarization training, and briefings, Thorne and his detachment were flown to the Special Forces camp at Chau Lang in IV Corps near the Cambodian border.

Thorne and his men could not believe their eyes when they arrived at Chau Lang. The camp looked like an old cavalry fort seen in a western movie, only much worse. Militarily, it was poorly sited in a miserable position with the region around the camp dominated by two mountains of the "Seven Mountains" where there was Viet Cong activity. The countryside around the camp was a Viet Cong stronghold of hardcore Communist activities harking back to the days of the Viet Minh. The only bright spot in this whole story was that the camp was manned by fierce Hoa Hao soldiers and Cambodians who had been recruited under the CIDG Program. The Hoa Hao, were ethnically Vietnamese, but belonged to a strange religious sect which fielded its own private army at one time.

Thorne found the Cambodians to be a valuable source of manpower and continually attempted to recruit them into his strike force. Not only were the Cambodians good fighters who provided valuable information from inside Cambodia, but they could be recruited in entire company-sized blocks with a built-in chain of command ready to lead. Many of the Cambodians were supporters of the Khmer Serei who had the objective of overthrowing Prince Sihanouk. Despite their politics, Thorne greatly admired the Hoa Hao and the Cambodians who he called his "little people" or "'Bodes" and they admired him.

On the other hand, he had only contempt for the South Vietnamese Special Forces officers who were assigned to Chau Lang. Through various political intrigues and plots, Thorne was able to have two weak or corrupt South Vietnamese Special Forces camp commanders relieved and replaced. He was eventually able to get one camp commander whom he could control and who was proficient as an officer. For most Special Forces camps, this was an rare accomplishment. Thorne's distrust of the Vietnamese Special Forces was so great that he took precautions in case of treachery. He went so far as to secretly place demolition charges in the Vietnamese fighting positions in case they turned against the Americans.

Detachment A-743's mission was very difficult. The Viet Cong dominated the local countryside, towns, and commerce through fear, intimidation, and coercion. The population was apathetic towards the Americans at best, and hostile at worst. Thorne found that the local "civil guards" rarely patrolled outside of their fort and had a sort of "gentleman's agreement" with the Communists whereby each side tended to mind their own business. Added to this, Thorne had problems with vicious Cambodian bandits who freely crossed the border to plunder any target of opportunity and cause mayhem.

Shortly after their arrival at Chau Lang, Thorne and his team were ordered to establish a new Special Forces camp in the nearby vicinity of Tinh Bien. Tinh Bien, a typical Vietnamese Mekong Delta town and district capital, was spread along a muddy canal which paralleled the Cambodian border. The site of their new camp was not much better than Chau Lang since the area was dominated by local mountains, and surrounded by flat, open rice paddies, crisscrossed with irrigation canals. Despite these tactical handicaps, Thorne once more accomplished his orders and established a Special Forces CIDG camp at Tinh Bien.

Detachment A-743 and their Hoa Hao/Cambodian CIDG strikers, fought through an almost constant ambush with the Viet Cong as they attempted to convoy the approximate 10 miles between Chau Lang and Tinh Bien. According to Thorne:

We had a four vehicle convoy and ran into a VC ambush. I was hit immediately—small fragments in both legs—but I was still able to move around okay.

I'd guessed the VC force numbered about 200 men and they were equipped with recoilless rifles and machine guns. There were only about 20 of us and 8 were wounded, but we fought for about an hour and a half, beat off two assaults and got away. I still don't know how I got out of that one alive.

After fighting their way to Tinh Bien and establishing the new camp, Thorne set about constructing his defensive positions within the camp and appealing to the local villagers to come and enjoy the "safety" of Tinh Bien. The Special Forces soldiers tried to improve the local economic status of Tinh Bien by purchasing local materials and hiring the local population to construct, develop and operate the camp. Although isolated, Team A-743 ran a medical dispensary; helped build a school and local market; initiated sanitation, agricultural and home improvement projects, improved the camp defenses, and conducted combat operations.

Captain Larry Thorne, Tinh Bien, Special Forces Camp, 1964 (Courtesy Mrs Kaija Mikkola).

The VC, angered by this bold intrusion into territory which they had controlled since the 1940s, exploited three major CIDG weaknesses:

1. Each Special Forces camp was on its own during the hours of darkness. Reinforcements were unlikely to arrive before daybreak if attacked at night.

2. The VC, through intimidation, could rely upon the villagers to remain silent thereby ensuring surprise. It was possible for a VC battalion-sized unit to move in close to the targeted camp and attack with complete surprise.

3. The VC infiltrated the CIDG camps posing as loyal villagers and strikers while providing intelligence and conducting sabotage.

The local Viet Cong entered into combat almost nightly with the defenders of Tinh Bien, or attacked Thorne's patrols when they left the perimeter of the camp. No quarter was given or taken by either side. It was a nerve-wracking process for the Special Forces soldiers. They never knew who they could trust. Sometimes, the VC dead were identified as nearby villagers or even traitorous strikers. Weapons and equipment had to be constantly checked against sabotage. Treachery and betrayal were constant companions for the small, isolated band of Americans. The battle for the pacification of the region was a slow and frustrating process. But Thorne, his detachment, and his "little people" were successful against the Viet Cong.

Thorne was not overly concerned about the Cambodian border and attacked the Viet Cong and Cambodian bandits whenever and wherever he found them. When possible, Thorne appealed to the Cambodian bandits' greed and bribed them with guns and money to attack the Viet Cong wherever they could find them. He used his Cambodian strikers to obtain intelligence about what was going on in Cambodia and attacked the Viet Cong when they were able to do so.

By early 1964, the situation in Tinh Bien had changed dramatically under Thorne's leadership. Houses and schools were built for the villagers who sought the safety offered by the Special Forces camp and shops were stocked full of goods for sale. The local farmers were no longer visited in the night by the Viet Cong or Cambodian bandits who took their rice, sons, and daughters. Viet Cong sampans no longer moved freely along the canals and the VC forces' mobility was severely hampered. Tinh Bien and its citizens thrived under the Special Forces' protection. But it was a long time before Thorne and the other Americans saw results. There was no finale at Tinh Bien, but they had started a trend which eventually broke the control of the Viet Cong in Chau Doc Province. In his book, *Inside the Green Berets,* Colonel Charles M. Simpson, III wrote that the scorekeepers and statisticians at MACV headquarters in Saigon did not view Tinh Bien as a success story. "What's happening at Tinh Bien?" queried a staff officer. "It used to be a really good camp with lots of body count. Now they hardly ever kill anybody!"

Added to the problems of the Viet Cong and the Cambodian bandits, Thorne had to deal with corrupt South Vietnamese Army officers and politicians in Saigon. Diplomacy and patience were not two of Thorne's strong characteristics. At one time, the South Vietnamese politicians feared that the Hoa Hao would assist a coup d' etat against the Saigon Government and quickly transferred 250 Hoa Hao strikers out of Tinh Bien. Thorne was livid with rage at this act, and accused the Saigon generals and politicians of being, "damned criminal stupid," but he was quickly muzzled by his American commanders who wished to maintain cordial relations with their South Vietnamese counterparts. It was a time of extreme political sensitivities and Thorne was held on a short leash. He was warned about his outbursts on numerous occasions and told to direct his comments only to trusted comrades.

In April 1964, Thorne and Detachment A-743 completed their 6-months TDY assignment at Tinh Bien and were replaced with another Special Forces team who began their TDY assignment. While Detachment A-743 had been at Tinh Bien, the author, Mr. Robin Moore, came and gathered material for a book he was writing about Special Forces. Thorne and his detachment's exploits at Tinh Bien were immortalized in Moore's best-selling novel, *The Green Berets*. Moore's novel and Barry Sadler's *The Ballad of the Green Berets* made Special Forces a household word in the United States. Even John Wayne's movie, *The Green Berets*, based upon Moore's book, attempted to portray the desperate fighting at Tinh Bien. But, Hollywood could not depict the true savagery or viciousness of the battles at the Special Forces border camps such as Tinh Bien.

In an interesting note, several months after Thorne's departure from Vietnam, Captain Roger H. Donlon won the Congressional Medal of Honor at the Special Forces Camp of Nam Dong during a desperate and costly fight as the VC attempted to annihilate the camp. Due to the almost constant fighting at Tinh Bien, every member of Detachment A-743 left Vietnam with at least one Purple Heart Medal for combat wounds. Thorne left Vietnam with two Purple Hearts and a Bronze Star Medal for valor. Upon his departure from Vietnam, Thorne knew that he would be back to fight the Communists.

17

INTERLUDE

Thorne returned to the 7th SFG(A) at Fort Bragg in May 1964. With the possibility of the US Army Reserves being called for service in Vietnam, it was critical to determine the level of training and readiness of the various Reserve Special Forces units.

A Major Compton, Captain Mike Phelan, and Thorne were tasked to proceed to Fort McClellan, Alabama to evaluate the 20th SFG(A) (Reserve) during field training. The entire exercise lasted approximately 18 days, and each evaluation was submitted to headquarters by approximately 1600 hours daily.

On one afternoon, Thorne returned to the headquarters in muddy jungle fatigues after spending the day evaluating field training to find his friend Mike Phelan working on his own evaluation report. Phelan had been evaluating the 20th SFG(A)'s headquarters and administrative activities and was dressed in his khaki Tropical Worsted uniform (TWs). After their reports were completed and submitted, Thorne and Phelan retired to the patio of a nearby Officer's Club to have a few drinks. While having their drinks, they noticed that several young, female officers were either sunning or swimming in a nearby pool. Both being single, Thorne noted that the swimming area was separated from the patio by a 4' retainer wall, and so the two friends began to dare each other to go swimming with the young ladies. With a few more drinks, a few false starts and more challenges, the race began over the wall and into the pool... muddy jungle fatigues, TWs and all.

Thorne, Phelan and the young ladies were having a great time laughing and splashing in the pool when the club manager, a Second Lieutenant, appeared and as sternly as possible, told the two Special Forces officers to get out of the pool. This request didn't go over very well with either Thorne or Phelan and they made their displeasure apparent to the young club manager who quickly disappeared. The young club manager took their suggestions literally and didn't return to bother them. After swimming for another leisurely 10 minutes, the two friends excused themselves from the young ladies, went back to their quarters, changed, and went into town to have dinner.

Early the next morning, the Post Commander had the commander of the 20th SFG(A)(Reserve) in his office and proceeded to verbally express his unhappiness with the conduct of the Special Forces commander's soldiers at the Officer's Club on the previous day. It was explained that the two culprits were not reservists, but were active duty evaluators! Rather than zero in on the two specific miscreants, the Post Commander served up his unbridled wrath upon the unfortunate Major Compton. The Post Commander was enraged not only because of the activities at the club, but also because he had started off by admonishing the wrong commander. Major Compton bore the full fury of the admonition without any excuses but later informed Thorne and Phelan that any other such actions would result in their permanent disbarment from

Fort McClellan. Thorne and Phelan looked contrite, but later laughed about the whole matter.

At the end of the evaluation period, Thorne returned to the 7th SFG(A) where he absorbed everything he could about Vietnam. Phelan ran into Thorne at Fort Bragg a short while later when he was assigned to help flesh out the 3rd SFG(A) after President Johnson announced that the reservists would not be activated. Phelan found Thorne once more relentlessly training an A-Team in preparation for deployment to Vietnam.

After receiving his new orders posting him to Vietnam, Thorne prepared to place all of his household goods into storage and move out of the small home that he was renting in Fayetteville, North Carolina. On his last evening before isolation in preparation for deployment, Thorne invited Phelan to his home in Fayetteville for steaks and a few drinks. For the rest of the evening, the two friends munched on the rosemary-impregnated steaks that Thorne loved and consumed bottles of beer, vodka, and peppermint schnapps as they laughed and talked.

"Hated to see it go to waste," said Phelan recently. The two friends watched as the sun came up heralding a new day. Thorne packed up the last of his household goods and proceeded to isolation at Camp Mackall while Phelan returned to his duties at the 3rd SFG(A). Each wished the other well and promised to see one another in Vietnam soon.

18

LAST MISSION

Something new was happening and Thorne was destined to become part of it. Returning to Vietnam for his second combat tour in February 1965, Thorne was assigned to the 5th Special Forces Group (Airborne) and initially served at various assignments on Phu Quoc Island, at Phuoc Vinh, and at Group Headquarters at Nha Trang. Phu Quoc was a large island in the Gulf of Siam just off of Cambodia. Covered with thick jungle, the VC used the island as a storage area and took enormous amounts of money from the inhabitants as "war taxes." Thorne and the Special Forces detachment attempted to deny the VC the use of the island as a supply and storage area. He was wounded for a third time as a Special Forces detachment commander in June 1965.

Through the 5th SFG(A), Thorne was funneled into their Special Operations Augmentation program, and then into an innocent sounding unit: Headquarters Company, Military Assistance Command Vietnam (MACV), Special Detachment 5891. Thorne had been recruited and accepted into the secret war. In reality, he had become a member of the Top Secret Military Assistance Command Vietnam—Studies and Observations Group (MACV-SOG). MACV-SOG was not a Special Forces unit, rather it was a MACV subordinate unit. Formed in secrecy in January 1964, MACV-SOG, was in reality, a joint service unconventional task force assigned to perform highly secret operations in a variety of specialties throughout Southeast Asia. Eventually, the special missions were only limited by the availability of transport to the target. Nearly all of MACV-SOG's operations remain classified to date.

From the very start, MACV-SOG attracted the best and most unorthodox officers and men in Special Forces. Its first commander, Colonel Donald Blackburn had led Filipino guerrillas against the Japanese during World War II. Blackburn, with the approval of Washington, formed Operations 35 (OP 35), which was also known as the Ground Studies Group. As the commander of OP 35, Blackburn named the legendary Colonel Arthur D. "Bull" Simons. He recently returned from the secret war in Laos (Operation White Star) and would later lead the Son Tay Prison Camp Raid in 1970. Thorne was recruited along with Major Sully Fontaine. Major Fontaine, a Belgian by birth, had served with the British SOE in Occupied Europe during World War II. Together, Thorne and the other officers recruited the volunteer Special Forces soldiers they needed and wanted for OP 35. With demanding standards, combat veterans from the 1st, 5th, and 7th Special Forces Groups (Airborne) who were no less than a Sergeant First Class (E-7) were recruited and sent for special training at Long Thanh, South Vietnam (Code named: BEARCAT). Many applied, but few were accepted.

At BEARCAT, Thorne's great experience gained in over 20 years of fighting the Communists was called upon to train the joint US Army and Vietnamese Special Forces teams for the tough and dangerous missions which lay ahead. Thorne's friends described him as being the ultimate soldier, but Thorne was exhausted. As one of his friends said later:

He (Thorne) had no wife, no family—he could never go home. I was a Major at the time, but I often deferred to him due to his extensive combat experience. I liked him the very first time I met him. His advice was invaluable.

Despite being 46 years old, Thorne could and regularly did, run his younger soldiers into exhaustion. Under Thorne's exacting standards, the teams were whipped into top physical shape and practiced their reconnaissance and combat skills until they were reflexive. Thorne had done this against the Russians, and his lessons were eagerly learned by his soldiers. Physical training began at the crack of dawn each day with plenty of running and calisthenics. After breakfast, there were at least two hours of weapons firing. The rest of the day was spent practicing team movements, tactics, and reconnaissance techniques.

Each team consisted of 10 to 12 men, normally composed of 2 or 3 Americans and the rest indigenous personnel. The number of team members could be smaller and the mix of men varied. The indigenous team members were often either Montagnard tribesmen or the fierce ethnic-Chinese Nung mercenaries. Their ages varied from as young as 15 to sometimes older than 40 years old. Indigenous team members' only allegiance was to the American team leader; however each team had an indigenous team leader who would report to the Americans and act as a go-between if there were problems. Each team had an interpreter, but the Americans quickly learned their team's language out of necessity. Experience showed that when the fighting started, the indigenous personnel would often revert to their native language and chaos ensued if the Americans could not speak the language.

The recon teams received special training in medical procedures, demolitions, communications, and photography. The medical training emphasized treatment for first aid, gunshot wounds; heat exhaustion and stroke, broken bones, snake bites, and the use of intravenous aid; i.e., plasma or albumin. Demolitions training centered around setting booby-traps, placing explosive charges for ambushes, and clearing helicopter landing zones. The Americans received extensive photographic training with both highly technical and simple cameras.

Team standard operating procedures (SOPs) were established so that every man on the teams knew their own and each other's duties and responsibilities, along with contingency plans. It was impressed upon the teams that their mission was for information, not killing North Vietnamese soldiers. Thorne faced other problems created by having joint teams. He knew that it was difficult to take the Vietnamese, put them in enemy territory, and expect them to perform like the American soldiers. Also, there was the matter of trust. It was easier for the Americans to trust the Vietnamese than it was for them to trust the Americans. Thorne and the other Americans had to convince the Vietnamese that they could take them into combat and bring them out alive. After every mission, the teams expected to participate in an extensive debriefing to learn about everything which had occurred during the mission. Polygraph (Lie Detector) tests were scheduled to be part of the debriefing. The Vietnamese team members were also advised that if the missions were not successful, they would not be paid.

Ultimately, Thorne and the Americans gained a special bond with the Vietnamese. None of the soldiers carried any identification; their maps were carefully trimmed and folded, while their equipment was from countries other than the United States. Not a single item of equipment from boots, socks, underwear, radios, weapons, or medical kits could be traced to American manufacture. Medical supplies were procured from Communist and neutral countries. Radio equipment was assembled from foreign components and even American medicines were transferred to foreign packaging. Although odd,

Thorne carried an obsolete, bolt-action Springfield M1903 rifle and was a deadly marksman with it. Other team members carried M-45 "Swedish K" submachine guns, M-1 & M-2 carbines, Browning Hi-Power 9mm pistols, and a variety of other foreign weapons. So many Springfield rifles and M-1/M-2 carbines were sold around the world that they were considered sterile. Each man knew that if they were killed or captured, both Washington and Saigon would absolutely deny any knowledge about them. As a graduation exercise, the teams of two Americans and four-to-ten South Vietnamese normally performed three reconnaissance missions in South Vietnam. After weeks of tough training, the teams were ready for deployment.

SFC David Kauhaahaa and indiginous team members board CH34 Kingbee helicopter on 2nd "Shining Brass" infiltration into Laos, October 1965, Kham Duc, SVN (Courtesy of David Kauhaahaa via John Larsen).

In September 1965, the infiltration of reconnaissance teams into Laos (Code named: SHINING BRASS) was approved, but was limited to no more than 50 kilometers into Laos. Washington imposed severe restrictions on the operations, but these restrictions were ignored in Vietnam by the use of deliberately inaccurate maps with errors as much as 10 kilometers to allow for quick, deep penetrations into enemy territory. In case the teams were captured, they were given flimsy cover stories to explain why they were operating in Laos. One cover story was that the teams had accidentally crossed into Laos looking for a crashed USAF C-123 cargo aircraft. In reality, these stories wouldn't have fooled the Communists and most team members expected to be executed or paraded around for propaganda value.

The first SHINING BRASS teams, one of which was composed of Master Sergeant Charles "Slats" Petry, Sergeant First Class Willie Card, one South Vietnamese Army Lieutenant and seven Nungs. They were deployed to the small Special Forces camp at Kham Duc which was being used as a Forward Operating Base (FOB) in preparation for their "launch" into Laos in search of what would be known as the "Ho Chi Minh Trail" or simply "The Trail."

The FOB at Kham Duc was located approximately 10 miles from Laos and was about midway along a 6,000 foot asphalt runway. Steep terrain covered with thick double—and triple—canopy jungle surrounded the camp which gave the impression of being in a green bowl with the camp located in the bottom. Kham Duc also sat beside national Highway 14 which paralleled the Laotian border and served as an avenue for the Communists to move from Laos towards the coastal plain around the major city of Da Nang. The FOB was commanded by Major Charlie Norton, an experienced and well-regarded Special Forces officer who did everything possible to support the recon teams. Petry's team was designated Recon Team Iowa. Four other Recon Teams (Idaho, Alaska, Kansas and Dakota) awaited their missions at Kham Duc.

The Trail allowed the North Vietnamese to move large quantities of troops and materials into South Vietnam. Finding and interdicting the Trail was a high priority for the South Vietnamese and Americans. The original launch date for Petry's team had been set for 15 October 1965. Unfortunately, it rained for three straight days. Thorne and his teams at Kham Duc remained in isolation and used the time checking and rechecking their equipment and memorizing their mission. Petry's team had been assigned to search an area identified as "D-1," approximately 20 miles northwest of Kham Duc, in Laos near the Laotian Highway 165.

The mission was reviewed over and over and memorized. All hygiene measures stopped several days before a team deployed since the smell of soap and deodorant lingered in the jungle for days. Camouflage sticks used to darken the reflective areas of the face were not used since the North Vietnamese did not use facial camouflage and would recognize those wearing it as enemy forces. Smoking was forbidden too. By the end of the third day, the men were rested and well fed. To the West lay Laos with a vague border, bad terrain, thick jungles with trees over 30 meters tall, and mountains which ranged from 1300 to 1800 meters high. Unknown to Thorne and his teams, the same area would be the scene of some of the fiercest small unit fighting and greatest bravery during the Vietnam War as the reconnaissance teams "went over the fence."

Late in the afternoon of 18 October 1965, the weather cleared enough for Thorne and Norton to launch the teams. It was determined that the importance of the mission outweighed the marginal weather being encountered. The South Vietnamese Air Force (VNAF), olive drab, unmarked Sikorsky CH-34 helicopters (Code named: KINGBEE), flown by the best helicopter pilots in the VNAF, headed West into Laos—and the unknown. Due to the hazards anticipated for this mission, a third helicopter was requested to fly along. Since Vietnamese aircraft were being used, there was a requirement that a US advisor fly along to ensure that maximum control was maintained. Headquarters also mandated a requirement that at least one American fly along to monitor the mission. Without hesitation, Thorne volunteered to fly along and to confirm the situation of the patrol on the ground prior to the helicopters' departure from the area. Thorne required that once on the ground, the patrol would report their landing and conduct a hasty security check of the landing area for enemy activity. He was familiar with the area since he had flown in many of the dangerous aerial reconnaissance missions prior to the start of Shining Brass operations.

Kham Duc FOB October 1965. CPT Larry Thorne, Major Emmons, MSG Charles "Slats" Petry, CPT Dinh (Kingbee Pilot) and "Cowboy" (Kingbee Pilot). (Courtesy of COL Charlie Norton via John Larsen).

Petry's team planned for a 5-day mission. They sat silently in the lead helicopter as the trail and Thorne's helicopter followed behind. They were soon joined in the air by a US Air Force single-engine Cessna O-1 Forward Air Controller (FAC) spotter aircraft flown by an Air Force major with a Marine Corps captain acting as an observer. The plan was for the lead and trail helicopter to land and drop off the reconnaissance team, while Thorne's helicopter and FAC remained above. If the reconnaissance team came under fire, or if something went wrong, Thorne's helicopter would act as a gunship while the other helicopters attempted to land and rescue the team.

Along the route to the landing zone, the helicopters received heavy ground fire from several locations. Arriving above the landing zone near sundown, the weather again closed in. Thick, angry clouds covered the LZ and the sun was going down quickly. The helicopters and the FAC circled the area looking for a way to get down. Just minutes before Thorne intended to cancel the mission and return to Kham Duc, the clouds opened up slightly. The lead and a trail helicopter dived into the cloud hole and unloaded Petry and his team without incident. As Thorne's helicopter and the FAC attempted to descend, the clouds again closed up. Thorne ordered the now empty lead and trail helicopter to return to Kham Duc.

Due to a heavy cloud bank, the helicopters were unable to return to Kham Duc along their planned route. Instead, they climbed to an altitude of 8,500 feet and circled while waiting for Thorne's helicopter. Within the several minutes that Thorne's helicopter had remained in the LZ area, the weather closed in completely around him. Disregarding his own personal safety, Thorne remained on station waiting for that critical patrol radio report thereby ensuring the safety of the reconnaissance team.

Finally receiving the patrol's satisfactory status report, Thorne's helicopter and the FAC attempted to fly out of the cloud banks. All their escape routes were obscured by the weather and spreading darkness. The two other helicopters continued to circle above waiting for Thorne and the FAC. Approximately five minutes after receiving the patrol's report, a constant keying lasting approximately 30 seconds was heard on the radio. Then silence. Neither Thorne nor the FAC answered the frequent radio calls made to them. Running out of fuel and with darkness falling, the other two helicopters waited and circled as long as they could. At the last possible moment, the two helicopters reluctantly turned and flew back to Kham Duc. At approximately 2020 hours, 18 October 1965, Captain Larry A. Thorne, three other men, a helicopter, and an aircraft disappeared into the mists of Laos. Tragically, they would be the first of many...

Intense searches were conducted for the next month, but with no results. Bad weather, enemy action, and rugged terrain ensured that Thorne's fate remained a mystery. Thorne's fate was determined after over 20 years of combat.

What of Petry's patrol? On the first night after being inserted, they moved away from the landing zone and set up a defensive perimeter. The heavy rains began again and continued on and off for the next five days.

For the next three days, the patrol struggled through the jungle where visibility was limited to ten meters or less and the mud was ankle deep. The rains made travel difficult and sleep impossible. Movement for the team was important. One Nung always walked point (lead man) and another as tailgunner (last man). If the team walked into an enemy patrol, the team members knew how to react to their challenge. At this moment of confusion training often saved many recon teams.

The team tried to walk through the jungle without leaving evidence of their passage such as torn vines, etc. Each man tried to step in the other's footprints and avoid areas which would create noise. Standard policy was for a recon team to move approximately one kilometer and then stop to listen for enemy movement or conversation. For all of their efforts, the patrol only moved approximately 15 kilometers in three days. But they soon heard their target, a truck park, in the distance.

The team found its target and noted fresh signs of North Vietnamese patrols operating around them. At the beginning of the fourth day, Petry briefed the team on what he wanted to do and moved the team away from the target.

As the team began to move, they were suddenly ambushed by the North Vietnamese. Petry's lead scout was killed instantly. Amid the firing, explosions and shouting, the other indigenous team members panicked. It was understood by all team members that if one of them went down to enemy fire, the team had to abandon him or out of mercy kill him. Recon teams which chose to stand and fight usually remained together—dead.

The North Vietnamese knew the military value of the recon teams and accepted terrible casualties to annihilate them. For them, the destruction of a recon team was considered a great victory. Petry and Card skillfully broke contact with the North Vietnamese, moved away from the ambush site and regrouped the team. Once the team regrouped, and leadership restored, Petry moved the team further away and called in an airstrike on the target.

Using his radio, Petry guided the jets onto the truck park. As the bombing continued, US Air Force jets found more and more targets. It was a frenzy of destruction. Meanwhile, Petry, carrying the dead Montagnard, led his team to a landing zone where they were lifted out of the jungle by helicopters and flown to Da Nang, South Vietnam. At Da Nang, the exhausted team was debriefed about every detail of their mission. As the facts became known, Blackburn, Simons, and Fontaine were pleased. Petry's team found the Ho Chi Minh Trail and called in a successful airstrike. But despite the celebrations, everyone was aware of the cost of Thorne's final mission.

At 1000 hours, 9 November 1966, a memorial service was held for Thorne at the US Army John F. Kennedy Center For Special Warfare (Airborne) Chapel at Fort Bragg, North Carolina. Earlier on 19 October 1966, the US Army declared that Captain Larry A. Thorne was no longer being listed as Missing-In-Action, but had been presumed Killed-In-Action in South Vietnam—not Laos. In fact, the Department of the Army stated, "On 18 October 1965, MAJ Thorne was a passenger aboard a Vietnamese Air Force CH34 helicopter which crashed about 25 miles south of Da Nang." As of 22 November 1995, the Department of the Army's POW/MIA Affairs Office still had him listed as Missing-In-Action, Presumptive Finding of Death.

Prior to his final mission, Thorne had been recommended for promotion to Major and was being groomed for a staff job as an intelligence officer. His posthumous promotion to Major was approved in December 1965. For his selfless actions in Laos, Thorne's family received a posthumous distinguished Flying Cross Medal.

The Törni family in Helsinki, Finland received the following letter of condolence:

Washington   3 November 1966

Dear Mr. Törni:

It is with deep sadness that I write to inform you that it has been necessary for the United States Army to issue a presumptive finding of death for your son, Major Larry A. Thorne, who has been missing in Vietnam since 18 October 1965. I assure you that this action has been taken only after our most exhaustive efforts to find out more about the circum-

stances of the disappearance of the helicopter on which your son was a passenger.

I know that the loss of a loved one is one of the most difficult things a person has to face, but perhaps you may find some measure of comfort in knowing that your son served his God and this country with courage and honor at a time of great need. The memory of his service will be treasured because he has joined the long line of soldiers who in times of peril have given their lives for freedom and for peace. In Vietnam today, as on other fields in earlier days, we are defending the right of men to chose their own destiny, the right of men to live in dignity and freedom. You can cherish the thought that you son was noble in giving his life to safeguard these blessings.

On behalf of the United States Army, I express heartfelt sympathy to you.

Sincerely,

Creighton W. Abrams
General, United States Army
Acting Chief of Staff

During the emotional memorial service, Chaplain (Major) Tom Cooley, along with Thorne's friends and fellow soldiers, remembered the adventures of his extraordinary life. Mrs. Hella Keravuori, the wife of one of Thorne's dearest friends, Colonel Aito Keravuori, recited a selection from *Vanrikki Stoolin Tarinat*, the poem, *"Alderkreuz."* With the music of *"Finlandia"* playing in the background, Mrs. Keravuori recited the national poem which ended with these words, "Here lives he, though there the grave." One of Thorne's subordinates and friend, Captain Bobby Evans later declared:

Larry was the best officer our unit has ever known. Special Forces lost in him its finest officer, the USA a great soldier, and the world, a magnificent man."

Major Larry A. Thorne's name is etched upon the copper memorial plate inside the Chapel, along with the names of hundreds of other Special Forces comrades who have died in the service of their country. On the wall of the Special Forces Memorial Court are engraved the words from the Bible, "I heard the Lord saying 'Whom shall I send and who will go for us...' Major Larry A. Thorne never failed to answer the call."

Thorne Memorial Service: L-R Mr. Peiti Eino, Törni's Father (Jalmari), Törni's sister (Salme), COL Matti Aarnio and US Army Military Attache (Courtesy of Lindholm-Ventola Family).

Thorne Memorial Service, Helsinki, 1966. Thorne's photograph, awards, and beret are on display (Courtesy of Lindholm-Ventola Family).

19

LEGACY

The Vietnamese have an interesting belief that a person can die more than once. Their belief is that a person dies a biological death; however, never dies a second time as long as his friends and family keep alive his memory. The circumstances of Thorne's disappearance only added to his legendary stature. There is a great deal of confusion regarding Thorne's disappearance.

Colonel Charles M. Simpson, III wrote in his book that the Kingbee crew members' remains were recovered at the crash site while Thorne's were not. Colonel Kairinen wrote in 1987, "All overflights in the area, planes and helicopters, were given orders for a continuous search for the location. But a positive identification was never made." In a more recent letter, Colonel Kairinen wrote, "During his second trip to Vietnam his airplane hit a high mountain and as the result, Larry A. Thorne perished in the crash."

Many of his friends refused to believe that he could be dead, and chose instead to believe that he not only survived the crash but would someday make his way out of the jungle.

Others have sought to believe that he somehow survived the crash, simply walked away from the war and is living somewhere incognito. One friend went so far as to say, "I wouldn't be surprised to learn that he's living in a cabin in Rovaniemi (Finland) with his feet up near a wood stove laughing his ass off at the rest of us." The vast majority of those who knew him have simply accepted and mourned his passing.

Could Thorne have survived? Could he have walked away from the crash and somehow made his way to Phnom Penh or Vientiane, and then returned to Europe? Possibly, since his life was full of unbelievable escapes. But why would he have gone to all the trouble to fake his own death just to walk away? Thorne knew that he could have walked into the 5th SFG(A) headquarters and asked for a non-combat job. He was 46 years old at the time of his disappearance and was exhausted. Except for Thorne himself, nobody else would have faulted him since his vast experience was more valuable in training others than in actual operations. Could he have survived the crash and been made a prisoner? This too is possible. The Soviet Union had not forgotten nor forgiven the humiliations that they had suffered at his hands. Recent revelations in Soviet documents and by former KGB General O. Kalugin have stated that selected American prisoners were sent to the Soviet Union during the Vietnam War for further interrogation. So far, Thorne's name has not been found or revealed as being in any Gulag.

During a conversation with one of Törni's nephew-in-laws, it was revealed that Törni's sister Kaija and family still believe that he is somehow alive. According to Mr. Jarl Törnquist, he heard that the search parties found Thorne's boot with a bone in it; however, he knew of no bone being found in the boot. Stranger still, Kaija, through Mr. Törnquist, revealed that she had received a simple drawing such as one done by street artists in 1982. The drawing showed the face of a man who would have been the same age as Thorne if he were alive and with similar features. It was posted from Las

Palmas, Spain, and was simply signed, "From a Friend." Could it have been a joke? Törni's relatives don't think so. Was it possible? The readers must decide for themselves.

Even in presumed death, Thorne's legacy as a superb soldier continued. In popular literature, Thorne was a character in Robin Moore's *The Green Berets*, and in Nicholas Proffitt's, *The Embassy House*. Historically, Thorne was mentioned in the Time/Warner Vietnam Experience Series, *War in the Shadows* and *A Contagion of War*; Jim Lucas' *Dateline: Vietnam,* COL Charles M. Simpson III's *Inside the Green Berets,* Shelby Stanton's *Green Berets at War* and John L. Plaster's *SOG: The Secret Wars of America's Commandoes in Vietnam.*

By the 1970s, Finland began to recognize the bravery and sacrifice of the members of the Asekätkenta and Törni. A Mr. Jukka Tyrkkö wrote a novel about Törni's life and adventures entitled, *Lauri Törnin tarina. Vapaustaistelijan vaiheita Viipurista Vietnamiin* (Lauri Törni's Story. Freedom Fighter From Viipuri to Vietnam). Tyrkkö maintained that he first met Törni in a Finnish Army hospital in 1944 when they were both recovering from wounds, and that he maintained contact with Törni until the late l950s.

Colonel Paavo Kairinen, one of Törni's dearest friends, retired from the US Army in 1972 and was able to return to Finland in 1982. Kairinen wrote an excellent history of the Asekätkenta and the 20 Finnish Officers who emigrated to America entitled, *Marttisen Miehet* (Marttinen's Men), and Törni was prominently mentioned. Mr. Antti Lindholm-Ventola, one of the original volunteers for the Osasto Törni wrote an excellent tribute to Törni in his book, *Lauri Törni ja hänen korpraalinsa* (Lauri Törni and His Corporal). On the direct orders of President Dr. Mauno Koivisto, Lars Rönnquist wrote an excellent history of the Osasto Törni entitled, *Törnin Jääkärit* (Törni's Jaegers). As Törni's former commander during the Continuation War, Rönnquist provided a detailed look at Törni and his unit's phenomenal exploits behind Soviet lines.

In 1971, the 10th SFG(A) was presented with a silver punch bowl by Thorne's former comrades-in-arms and others who wished to honor his memory. This beautiful punch bowl is engraved with the crossed flags of Finland and the United States, with Master Parachutist Wings and the crest of the 10th SFG(A)—the Trojan Horse insignia affixed. Each individual punch cup is engraved with the names of the recipients of the Larry Thorne Award. The award was created to recognize and reward the most outstanding operational detachment in the Special Forces line battalions and the most outstanding support section or platoon. Specific program goals were developed to:

A. Recognize the collective superior efforts of individuals toward a team mission.
B. Promote morale and espirit de corps.
C. Symbolize team effort and teamwork.

The Thorne Cup Award (individual cups not shown) (Courtesy of SGT Gregory Hector, HGS., 10th SFG (A)).

A special ceremony is conducted by the Group Commander to present the Larry Thorne Award. The recognized unit receives a letter and certificate as well as a silver cup inscribed with each member's name symbolizing the award of the Larry Thorne punch bowl. All silver cups are donated by field grade (Major and above) and promotable Captains upon their departure from the Group. The individual benefits to this team achievement are varied:

1. A four day pass.
2. A formal letter and certificate to each individual to be placed in official files.
3. Special efficiency reports for the officer and senior NCO supervisors.

Every presentation of the Larry Thorne Award is a special occasion. It is a time when the outstanding efforts of a team towards a team mission are recognized. The tradition continues and the punch bowl is on permanent display at the 10th SFG(A) Group Headquarters.

In 1983, the Special Operations Association (SOA), established a scholarship in memory of Thorne, the Special Operations Association's first listed Missing-In-Action casualty, for the children of the men who have served their country in special operations. The first recipient was Benjamin S. Redman of Norwalk, Iowa, whose father, Darrell Redman served with Command and Control, Central, MACV-SOG.

In 1986, the XXXIII Chapter of the Special Forces Association was renamed in honor of Major Larry A. Thorne. According to the then Chapter President, Mr. Bobby R. Burke, "In this way, we hope that his outstanding defense of freedom will not be forgotten."

Every year, the 80 some surviving veterans of the Osasto Törni (as of 1992) gather annually to honor their former commander and comrades. These veterans served in the Osasto

Törni at various times. As of 1991, only one of the original members was still alive. Recently, the President Emeritus of Finland, the Honorable Dr. Mauno Koivisto, who served as a 19 year-old sniper and light machine gunner in the Osasto Törni in 1944, hosted the annual reunion at his summer residence. Looking at the old and frail men in the reunion photos, it is sometimes hard to believe that these same men were once the terror of the Red Army. But one only has to look into the eyes of these men to see the toughness and determination which kept Finland free. Many still openly weep in remembrance of Lauri Törni and their fantastic missions. Former Corporal Antti Lindholm-Ventola made an interesting observation before he died. In some of his last lines, he wrote:

One may ask how Törni's men did in civilian life? They have proven their quality also in civilian life as skilled workers, and professionals; i.e., economists, engineers, judges, doctors, and even the present President of Finland (Dr. Mauno Koivisto). We, Törni's men are aged people. The joys and sorrows of our prime years are behind. Now, there is time to remember the past and keep in touch with each other. Those of us, members of Törni's unit, who have been in touch with you, sir, have tried to show you about our continuing activity.

The 79th graduating class of Finland's Military Academy in 1995 chose Törni as their class symbol and inspiration. These young, graduating officers recognized the fighting spirit and unyielding dedication of Kapteeni Lauri Törni to represent their class. Hopefully, they will emulate the dedication which Törni showed and defend their homeland with the same ferocity that Törni displayed throughout his entire lifetime. Ironically, it has gone full circle, from conscript to national hero, to accused traitor, and once again a national hero. Could any man or storyteller have ever dreamed of such a life, let alone dare to live it?

Oil painting of Captain Thorne in the Zagros Mountains. Now hanging in the 10th SFG (A) Headquarters. (Courtesy of SGT Gregory Hector, HQS, 10th SFG (A)).

COL Lambert and CSM Janis dedicate the new 10th SFG (A) Headquarters at Fort Carson, CO on 26 July 1996. "Thorne Hall" (Courtesy of 10th SFG (A)).

Besides having Thorne's name engraved on the copper plate in the JFK Special Warfare Chapel, Thorne's name is also engraved at the Vietnam War Memorial, "The Wall." His name is engraved on Plate 2E, Line 126, surrounded by the approximately 58,000 other comrades-in-arms who perished in that conflict. Few, if any, can visit that memorial and fail to be moved by the enormity of sacrifice.

Finally, the US Army moved the headquarters of the 10th SFG(A) from Fort Devens, Massachusetts to Fort Carson, Colorado in 1995. A new headquarters building was constructed, along with other support structures. Early on it was decided that the new headquarters should be named in honor of Major Larry A. Thorne. The dedication was finally held on 26 July 1996, when the 10th SFG(A) Group Commander, Colonel Geoffrey Lambert and SGM Gerald Janis unveiled a bronze plaque naming the new headquarters the "CPT Larry A. Thorne Building." The small ceremony was held shortly before Colonel Lambert's change of command and rated only a small notice in the Chapter News section of the Special Forces Association magazine, *The Drop*. A larger, more formal ceremony, is pending to date.

Lauri A. Törni/Larry A. Thorne, was just a man, not a god or an idol. He was a hero, albeit an imperfect one.

APPENDIX I

TÖRNI /THORNE'S AWARDS

AMERICAN AWARDS
Legion of Merit Medal (Posthumously)
Distinguished Flying Cross Medal (Posthumously)
Bronze Star Medal
Purple Heart Medal with 3 Oak Leaf Clusters
Air Medal (Posthumously)
Army Commendation Medal
Good Conduct Medal
National Service Medal
Vietnam Campaign Medal
Vietnam Service Medal
Combat Infantryman's Badge
Master Parachutist Badge

FINNISH AWARDS
Mannerheim Risti 2lk (Mannerheim Cross)
Vaupaudenristi 4tlk (Freedom Cross, 4th Class)
Vaupaudenristi 4mk (Freedom Cross 4th Class -
lower grade)
Vaupaudenristi 3mk (Freedom Cross 3rd Class)
Vaupaudenmitali 2lk (Freedom Medal 2nd Class)
Vaupaudenmitali 1lk (Freedom Medal lst Class)
Muistomitali 39-40 (Winter War Medal 1939-1940)
Muistomitali 41-44 (Continuation War Medal 1941-
1944)
* Wounded three times (no award given)

GERMAN AWARDS
Iron Cross, 2nd Class

VIETNAMESE AWARDS
    Special Forces Parachutist Badge

APPENDIX II

AFTERMATH

MARTTINEN'S MEN

As the provisions of the Peace of Moscow came into being, some senior members of the Finnish General Staff made secret provisions of their own. These officers knew that the Soviet's demands were direct threats to Finland's independence and sovereignty. Additionally, they knew that they could only count on themselves, not their Western Allies, to defend their nation. Soviet treachery had become apparent due to the invasions of Romania and Hungary after they had signed similar armistices with the Soviets. As the Finnish Army returned to the 1939 manning levels, the highly secretive **Asekätkenta** (Arms Hiders), began to establish caches of weapons and military supplies throughout Finland in violation of the Peace of Moscow. In a military sense, the caching of weapons was a practical one; however, politically, it was open to risk and criticism. If the Soviet Union needed a formal reason to occupy Finland, the Asekätkenta's actions provided one. Still, the Asekätkenta went about obtaining and hiding light weapons, ammunition, communications, equipment, and clothing necessary to outfit a guerrilla force of approximately 34 battalions of 600 - 800 men each ready to fight an underground war if the Soviets invaded. The members of the Asekätkenta were under no illusions. They intended to make the expected Soviet occupation very costly.

Aided by trusted non-commissioned officers and civilians, the patriots of the Asekätkenta quietly moved weapons and material from depots to secret caches around the country while providing guerrilla warfare training. The Asekätkenta established a command structure, organization and communications to coordinate the expected guerrilla war. So well hidden and secretive were these caches that they are still being discovered to this day.

With each passing day, the Asekätkenta watched as Communist sympathizers, radicals, and opportunists entered the Finnish government and police; especially the State Police (Valpo). These Communist watchdogs soon heard rumors of the preparations of the Asekätkenta and quickly bowed to the wishes of their Soviet masters. Saying that they had to take action, rather than risk the intervention of the Soviets, these Communist sympathizers in the government and police soon discovered their secret operation and the ambitious plans. The Soviets were also aware of the Asekätkenta's activities, but used their Finnish lackeys to do the dirty work.

A reign of terror, fear, and intimidation soon fell upon Finland as the Communist sympathizers arrested some 2000 Asekätkenta members. Roundups, brutal interrogations, and imprisonment without charges became the order of the day. The Valpo dismantled "fascist organizations" and groups deemed to be subversive. Sentences of up to 10 years in prison were routinely handed out at massive anti-fascist and war crimes trials. Threatened with arrest and imprisonment for their efforts to defend Finland, many of the Asekätkenta sought to flee Finland and seek freedom. Beginning in 1945, the exodus began. Many of these patriots were not able to return to their homeland for many years to come.

Some escaped just in time. One member escaped after receiving a whispered telephone call from a friend warning that the Valpo was on their way to his home at that very minute. By various routes, many of the Asekätkenta escaped Finland to nearby Sweden. For approximately two years, these Finns were stateless persons, unable to leave and yet unable to return home. Sometimes taking work as lumberjacks, etc., they bid their time until they could somehow get to the United

States. Finland soon pressured the Swedish Government to force these potentially troublesome Finnish refugees to return to Finland and their arrests. The Swedish resisted and bought precious time for the refugees. Despite the political discussions, Sweden was still a dangerous place for the Asekätkenta members. On one occasion, members of the Soviet embassy staff attempted to kidnap a member of the Asekätkenta on a busy Stockholm street in daylight using a clearly marked Soviet embassy automobile. The Finn escaped. In the meantime, one of their members, Colonel Alpo K. Marttinen, gingerly contacted the United States Government to arouse interest in their plight. In 1945, Field Marshal Mannerheim told Marttinen, "Your only hope is the United States. Try to get there. You are needed still!" Colonel Marttinen, the youngest Colonel in the Finnish Army, a hero of the battle of Suomussalmi, and a Knight of the Mannerheim Cross (Finland's Medal of Honor), suggested to the Americans:

> ...that we recruit, say, a couple of thousand war-hardened Finnish officers and aid their transportation to America and form units from them in the US Army...As soon as they learn the English language and become familiar with US Army tactics, we will get extraordinary material for our army's use in northern battlefields. At the same time they would be a possible force in Finland's fight against Soviet absorption, because the Finnish officer corps can thus be preserved under the colors of the United States.

Thus, Marttinen was able to gain the support of the US Government to assist members of the Asekätkenta in immigrating to the United States. Some twenty Finnish Army officers and their families were able to follow Marttinen from Sweden, through Venezuela and into the United States while traveling on Nansen (stateless persons) passports.

Arriving in the United States by various routes and means, these Finnish officers become common laborers, etc., to survive. These were tough times as the FBI thoroughly investigated the Finn's backgrounds to determine whether they were to remain in the United States and suitable for the US Army. But, Marttinen now had powerful allies such as General William C. Wedemeyer and Senator Arthur Vandenburg and the Cold War had added concern to his dire predictions regarding the Soviets.

The twenty members of the Finnish group, after being deemed suitable and allowed to join the US Army in 1947, as privates, were no longer the senior officers that they had previously been in the Finnish Army. Their lives and circumstances were still difficult, but they continued to make the best of the situation. Private Marttinen had gotten the US Army interested in winter warfare and offered his fellow Finns as the best instructors available. By 1948, the Finns had proven their military worth, were learning English and were promoted to non-commissioned ranks. Reassigned, the Finns became scattered throughout the US Army. Master Sergeant Marttinen became the first and only enlisted instructor at the US Army Command and General Staff College at Fort Leavenworth, Kansas—this while his American instructor counterparts were Lieutenant Colonels.

By 1950, Marttinen had recommended that all the Finns be promoted to reserve officer ranks. He continued to make the point that the US should help more Finns to escape and that war between the West and the Soviet Union was inevitable. The conflict in Korea soon bolstered Marttinen's argument for the formation of a "Liberty Legion" along with further winter warfare training. Unfortunately for Marttinen's vision, Congress passed the Lodge Act which gave citizenship to individual refugees from Communism rather than whole drafts of ethnic groups.

Congress approved Marttinen's request for promotion to officer rank for the Finns; however, they remained on active duty status as NCOs, with reserve commissions. After being called to active duty as regular commissioned officers, the fourteen Finns' status changed in 1951. Marttinen became a Lieutenant Colonel while the others received promotions to Majors, Captains and Lieutenants.

Through clandestine communications, Marttinen continued to entice Finnish officers who had remained behind to defect to the United States. Soon several other Finns, including the legendary Lauri Allan Törni (later Major Larry Allan Thorne), also a Knight of the Mannerheim Cross, fled to the United States. While Marttinen's dream of a Nordic legion died due to other pressing concerns and political faintheartedness, the record of these Finnish soldiers stands.

Over the next twenty years, these Finns served throughout the US Army in a variety of demanding duties. All provided exemplary service to their adopted country; many served in combat in Korea and Vietnam or with Special Forces. Seven of the Marttinen Men, as they became known, retired as Colonels and four retired as Lieutenant Colonels. Colonel Marttinen would have allegedly been promoted to Brigadier General had he been younger. Lieutenant Colonel Olavi Alakulppi, also a Knight of the Mannerheim Cross, had been a world class skier and freely taught his knowledge of winter warfare to the US Army, and later to the US Olympic Team. Colonels Aito Keravuori and Paavo Kairinen were both veterans of extensive combat against the Red Army and served admirably in Special Forces. Colonel Kalle Keranen served with distinction in both the Korean War and Special Forces.

There was sacrifice too. Major Larry Thorne provided legendary service in Special Forces, although later declared missing-in-action, presumed dead during an early MACV-SOG operation into Laos. Colonel Marttinen's oldest son, Lieutenant Pekka Marttinen, perished with his tank crew in a gunnery explosion at Grafenwöhr, Germany in 1959. Lieutenant Vesa Alakulppi, the son of LTC Olavi Alakulppi, graduated from The US Military Academy at West Point, only to die in action in Vietnam in 1967.

America came very close to having a true Foreign Legion in the 1950s. The Marttinen Men, along with the thousands of other foreign born patriots who joined the US military under the Lodge Act served their adopted nation well. In the case of the Marttinen Men, it should be the memory of their courage, spirit, determination, and sacrifice which gives true meaning to the phrase, "Land of the Free and Home of the Brave."

MARTTINEN'S MEN BY NAME:

Marttinen, Alpo K.
Aakkula, Antero
Kairinen, Paavo
Keravuori, Aito
Keranen, Kalle
Lahdenpera, Erkki
Lasila, Eino
Alakulppi, Olavi
Patojarvi, Erik
Vikstrom, Arvo
Nysten, Pauli
Paivarinne, Anto
Saastamoinen, Toivo
Turtiainen, Teuvo
Antilla, Juho
Sinkko, Onni
Uitto, Sulo
Jarvinen, Vesa
Pihala, Olavi
*Törni , Lauri

* Törni was not an original member of the group of Finnish officers who immigrated to the United States in 1947.

APPENDIX III

NOTES REGARDING MACV-SOG

More information is being released about MACV-SOG. The citizens of the United States will be amazed about these valiant men and their deeds. They truly were "The Quiet Professionals."

Major John L. Plaster, US Army, Retired, was a former MACV-SOG Recon Team member who recently wrote a book entitled, *SOG: The Secret Wars of America's Commandoes in Vietnam.*

Some highlights of MACV-SOG activities are outlined below:

1. OP 35, Ground Studies Group ran approximately 3,000 missions into Laos, Cambodia, and North Vietnam during the Vietnam War.

2. Exact casualties for MACV-SOG were hidden in other units' casualty reports during the Vietnam War.

3. Casualty rates for MACV-SOG have been estimated at approximately 200%, with a fatality rate of approximately 70%—yet, there was never a shortage of volunteers. Unofficially, MACV-SOG had 103 dead—76 were said to be killed in Laos with another 27 killed in Cambodia. These numbers do not include the South Vietnamese, Nung, and Montagnard team members' casualty numbers.

4. Of the approximately 2,500 American servicemen reported as Missing-In-Action during the Vietnam War, 53 were MACV-SOG recon team members.

5. Of the 17 Special Forces soldiers awarded the Congressional Medal of Honor, 5 were MACV-SOG, OP 35 members.

6. Kingbee pilots were members of the 216th Vietnamese Air Force Squadron and considered to be hot helicopter pilots. These brave men took amazing risks to support the

recon teams who "went over the fence." Several years ago, the author met a former Kingbee pilot, now living in Orange County, California, who had been shot down five times, been horribly burned, and lost one of his hands in his last crash. After the fall of South Vietnam, the Communists imprisoned this heroic man in a "Re-Eduction Camp." He somehow escaped with his family and came to the United States. After all of this, he proudly and happily reminisced about "his recon teams." According to him, no landing zone was too dangerous if a team called for help. He considered the recon team members, "The bravest men I have ever known."

7. The late Colonel Charlie Beckwith, former commander of Project Delta and Special Forces Operational Detachment - Delta, and a man not known for giving praise or kind words lightly, once said of the Kingbees: "They were some of the bravest men I'd ever met. They were handpicked, the cream of the Vietnamese Air Force, and they were the finest pilots in the country."

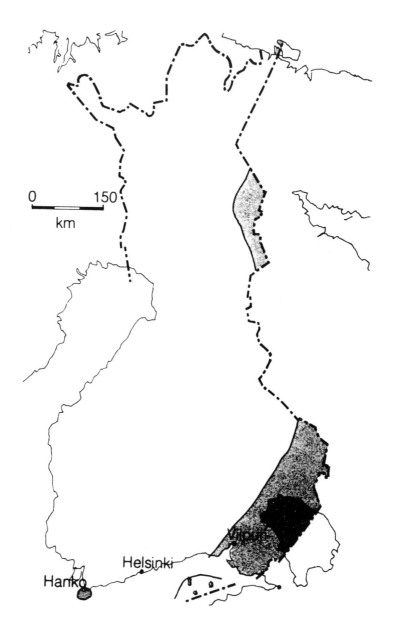

Ceded areas of Finland after Winter War.

APPENDIX IV

VIIPURI AFTER THE WAR

The invading Soviets occupied Törni's hometown of Viipuri in March 1940. The Finns regained the city at the beginning of the Continuation War in 1941, but lost it when the Soviets reoccupied the city in 1944. The original city of Viipuri was a mass of twisted rubble and destruction.

Since 1944, the Soviet Union did little to rebuild the city to its former beauty and grandure. Before the Winter War, Viipuri was Finland's second largest city and a thriving seaport and marketplace. Neo-Stalinist soulless gray concrete buildings, drab apartment buildings, and statues of Lenin replaced Viipuri's beautiful architecture.

The surrounding abandoned cities and farms were occupied by thousands of Soviet citizens, imported from Russia, the Ukraine and Kyrgystan. Viipuri, along with Karelia, was stripped of natural resources and severely polluted.

With the demise of the former Soviet Union and the relaxation of tensions along the Soviet-Finnish frontier, many of the 400,000 displaced Finnish citizens streamed back towards Viipuri and the surrounding area. This time they came as tourists in search of their past rather than as refugees fleeing for their safety. What they found after 1992 was unsettling. Young Russians begged for spare change, sold bottles of black-market vodka, and sold religious icons. The Finns were saddened by the physical and moral decay of Viipuri. The Finns found their former city occupied by approximately 250,000 Russians; many of them, 2nd generation citizens.

Fifty years of Soviet occupation irrevocably changed the city of Viipuri. Vandalized, the old city cemetery was abandoned and overgrown with weeds. The Soviets pulled down the statue of the city's Swedish founder and numerous old churches and historical sites became warehouses and shops. A park now stands where the Communists had obliterated the Finnish war cemetery. The Soviets desecrated the Finnish soldiers' graves by piling layers of dirt over the sites and headstones when the area was changed to a "Worker's Park." In an attempt to heal some of the wounds, the Russians have recently erected a simple wooden cross with the following inscription in Finnish, German, Swedish, and Russian:

"Dedicated to the memory of all those buried in Vyborg."

The Finns pumped money and professional aid into Viipuri in an attempt to restore some of the old buildings. The Lutheran Church of Peter and Paul, on the city commons, was returned to its former glory after the Soviets made it into a dance hall.

Viipuri and the lost Finnish territories continues to be a source of friction between Finland and the former Soviet Union. The older generation of Finns still believe that Finland should recover the land lost to the Russians while later generations are more pragmatic about the problem. While Finland and the Russians have signed a treaty to increase their mutual cooperation regarding Karelia, there are many questions that remain. Having viewed Germany's problems and costs associated with their reunification, the Finns are leery of regaining formerly Communist-controlled territory. Since the area remains occupied by Russians, Finland does not want to regain territory that does not have a Finnish population. Then there is the pollution and environmental problems created by the Russians. Finally, there is the question of who would pay for such a reunification?

INDEX

Valli, 59
Valpo, 75, 85-87, 103
Vandenburg, Arthur, 102
Vanrikki Stoolin Tarinat, 174
Veterinarian NCO Academy, 22
Vietnam, 9, 107, 137-138, 151-152, 158, 161-162, 167, 173-174, 177
Vietnam War, 168, 178
Vietnam War Memorial, 184
Vietnamese Special Forces, 163
Vigorg, 144
Viipuri (Vyborg), 19-21, 32, 68
Viipuri Business High School, 19, 21
Viipuri Grammar School, 19
von dem Bache, 69
W
Waffen SS, 36-38, 68-69, 71, 75, 82, 101
Waffen SS: The Asphalt Soldiers, 37
War in the Shadows, 179
Wars of National Liberation, 136
Warsaw, 71
Wayne, John, 158
Wedemeyer, William C., 102
Wellington, 54
Werfulf Organization, 65-78
West Point, 121
West German Intelligence, 74
Wheeler, Jim, 8-9
Winter War, 29-32, 35, 42-44, 64-65, 96
World War I, 45, 100
World War II, 64, 82, 95, 100, 107, 142, 163
Y
Yalta Conference, 79

ORDER FORM

TO:
Pathfinder Publishing
458 Dorothy Ave.
Ventura, CA 93003
Telephone (805) 642-9278   FAX (805) 650-3656
Book Ordering Number (800) 977-2282

Please send me the following books from Pathfinder Publishing:

_____ Copies of **Elite Warriors** Hard Cover, @ $22.95 $_____
_____ Copies of **Silent Warriors** @ $22.95 $_____
_____ Copies of **Surviving a Japanese P.O.W. Camp**
      @ $9.95 $_____
_____ Copies of **Agony & Death on a Gold Rush Steamer**
      @ $8.95 $_____
_____ Copies of **Shipwrecks, Smugglers & Maritime**
      Mysteries @ $9.95 $_____
_____ Copies of **Soldier Under Three Flags** @ $14.95 $_____
                                      Sub-Total $_____

      Californians: Please add 7.25% tax. $_____
      Shipping* $_____
                                        Grand Total $_____

I understand that I may return the book for a full refund if not satisfied.
Name:_____

Address:_____
_____ZIP:_____

Credit Card: Visa_____ Master_____
No._____

*SHIPPING CHARGES U.S.
Books: Enclose $3.25 for the first book and .50c for each additional
book. UPS: Truck; $4.50 for first item, .75c for each additional.

THE AUTHOR

H.A. Gill, III, is a graduate of The Citadel with a B.A., Cum Laude with Department Honors in History. Serving in the US Army as an infantry officer, he attended numerous military speciality schools with assignments in both CONUS and overseas. As a freelance writer and researcher, he has written numerous magazine and newspaper articles on military history and affairs in the United States and internationally. He currently resides in California with his wife and children where he works for a major aerospace coporation.